Socially Challenged

Millie Hoelscher Moran

P*

POLARIS PUBLICATIONS
An imprint of NORTH STAR PRESS OF ST. CLOUD, INC.
St. Cloud, Minnesota

Copyright © 2012 Millie Hoelscher Moran

First Edition: November 2012

Printed in the United States of America

Printed by Polaris Publications
An imprint of:
North Star Press of St. Cloud, Inc.
P.O. Box 451
St. Cloud, Minnesota 56302

northstarpress.com

Dedication

This writing endeavor is gratefully dedicated to my parents, Henry and Lucille Hoelscher and their families, the Benedictine Sisters who staffed the Browerville parochial school and St. John's Hospital, the physicians, medical personnel, hospital staff and especially the patients and their families who were the educational link for me between elementary school and my wedding day, my acquired California family and all individuals who have been life experience teachers in my forty years back in Minnesota. I thank God for each of you, who have taught me more than I ever dreamed possible.

Socially Challenged

*Bob & Bobbie
You are precious!
Mellie Hoelscher Moran
& Don Too.*

Introduction

Why now? Why strive to write a book at this point in my life? Writing has been my passion although I've never been serious about getting a book published. Last year I was diagnosed with memory loss consistent with possible onset of Alzheimer's disease and am taking the prescribed drug Namenda. Writing might assist in working with the drug by helping to stimulate brain neurons. Likewise, in this time in history when the United States and world economies are nearing the Great Depression status, some of my children and their families are in dire financial straits. This project could serve as a healthy diversion for my concerned parent/grandparent disposition.

In the summer of 2011, two registered nurses who were my supervisors over fifty years ago and I decided to pack our seventy-something bodies into my vehicle that accommodates my physical limitations. We headed north three hours from Eagle Bend, Minnesota to Crookston, Minnesota to have lunch with our eighty-one year old former nurse anesthetist supervisor, Sister Jacquelyn. We must be risk takers. It was the highest heat index day of the summer, 103 degrees. In addition, we had no idea of how one another's personalities had evolved during the past half-century and yet we three chose to spend six hours together in a vehicle for the journey. Our sweet, angelic Sister Jacquelyn hosted us for a few hours of life in a monastery with retired sisters who managed to keep busy smiling while being in a primarily non-air conditioned facility.

During lunch other sisters stopped to chat with us and asked if I was a nurse too. I disclosed that I was a nurse's aide who had lived an isolated existence on a farm near Browerville and that these three women were instrumental in guiding me through experiences in a hospital setting there. They cushioned my transition from being socially naïve to cautiously taking the calculated risk of leaving my protective farm family life and environment for life in Los Angeles, California.

Those who lived and worked with me might read this account and say, "It wasn't like that at all." They may be right. Some names of characters have been changed to respect the innocent and guilty as well. Some embellishing or diminishing of situations was used to aid in the imagery and flow of the story. This is not meant to be an absolute account of facts. It is, however, creative non-fiction, the truth as perceived through the eyes and ears of a young naïve country bumpkin who continues to be committed to meeting challenges far beyond her training for situations. The result: An adventurous and fulfilling life.

Chapter One

In 1938, few rural Minnesota hospitals existed. However, Todd County, in central Minnesota, was blessed with three. These aging medical facilities appeared to be modest, oversized, turn-of-the-century to-1920 two-story houses. The three early hospitals were located in Long Prairie—the county seat—Bertha, and Staples. Babies were usually delivered at the mother's home. Most often a doctor was present. I, however, was born in the original Bertha Hospital. It was twenty miles from the farm near Browerville which my German immigrant grandparents homesteaded, and where I grew up.

As the story was told to me, my parents lived with my dad's parents for seven months, with their upstairs bedroom and Uncle Glen's bedroom separated by a sitting room. My dad anticipated raising a family that would assist with farming. Thinking they may not have children, my parents considered adopting a child.

Mom told of this being a difficult period for her. Dad's family spoke German and Mom, who spoke only English, felt like an outsider. Dad informed his family that when Mom was present, they were to speak English.

His family complied. When the newlywed couple eventually moved to the neighboring farm, also owned by Grandpa, Mom became pregnant with me almost immediately.

Prior to marriage, my mother was a farm girl, or more of a tomboy. She had one older and two younger sisters before the arrival of brothers. While she envied the relationship her older sister had with their mother, she often reminisced of the joy she experienced working with her dad on the farm. While living with in-laws was difficult, nineteen year old Lucille learned the art of homemaking from her mother-in-law.

Story has it that in my Mom's seventh month of pregnancy, she was kicked in the abdomen by a cow. Bleeding resulted and Mom was bedridden for the two months prior to my birth. As an adult, I asked Mom if she occupied herself with reading during those months with me kicking inside of her. She responded, "No, I just laid so happy knowing that I was cooperating with God to bring a new life into the world." Due to possible complications, her physician, Dr. Gross, wanted her to deliver in the Bertha Hospital, where he was on-staff. Apparently all went well. As was customary at the time, the mother and newborn were discharged nine days later. The first frost was late that year. Blooming gardens turned brown during the nine-day confinement period.

Mom descended from a generation when pregnant women, especially those unable to conceal their condition in their final trimester, refrained from attending church services. In their minds, the presence of a woman with child would distract from the solemnity of sacred liturgies. In the earlier generation, when a priest was called to the home to give the Last Rites of the Catholic Church to a dying parishioner, obviously pregnant women would not answer the door upon the priest's arrival. They remained in the background. Circumstances of pregnancies were hush-hush in that era. Miscarriages were not talked about.

****

The next three arrivals in my family were boys born thirteen to fourteen months apart and delivered by Doctor Gross at our home. The four of us were born within three-and-a-half years. While too young to remember anything of Linus invading my center of the universe status, I know that during the arrival of Harry, the second boy, Grandma Becker assisted the doctor. After the birth, Grandpa Becker, Mom's dad, informed his tomboy daughter that Grandma would be unable to assist with childcare the following weeks. Only then did Mom learn that her mother was due to deliver a baby soon. Mom was twenty-three years old and had no idea that her mother was seven months pregnant. Grandma's new baby girl became my playmate, who also moved into the cutest little girl category in the family.

    I remember when the fourth child was about to be born, we three older siblings were whisked off in the middle of the night to our grandparent's home next door. I cozied up in bed between Grandma and

Socially Challenged

Grandpa Hoelscher, who were also my godparents. In the morning, Uncle Glen informed his parents that one of the little boys sleeping with him had wet the bed. When we returned home I was allowed to hold newborn Eugene.

Some months later Mom learned that she was pregnant with twins. This time the new Doctor Lenarz, in Browerville, was their doctor of choice. He and his wife, Kathryn, had moved to town to open a clinic. His youth, compassion, and dedication appealed to the people of Browerville and the surrounding communities. In the beginning Dr. Lenarz took patients to neighboring hospitals. Grandma Hoelscher had transferred to the new physician as well. She died of leukemia in December of 1942. That meant she would not be available to assist the family with the upcoming twin births.

Grandma's cold—hard—body rested in a casket near the window in what was a farm formal dining room. I remember so many people coming for the visitation and their chuckles when two-year-old Harold proclaimed; "I see Bammer . . . I see Bammer." An adult would lift him up to see the deceased Hoelscher family matriarch. I enjoyed watching my younger brothers. My grandmother/godmother was gone and I had just turned four years old. Uncle Glen was still single. My female mentors were nearly non-existent. I was just a kid already taking on heavy adult concerns and emotions.

In the middle of a March snowstorm in 1943, Mom, experiencing contractions, thought it was time to leave for the hospital. With low visibility and unable to see the road ahead of them, Dad and Mom followed a snowplow to the Bertha Hospital. False labor pains meant Mom returned home. The storm was followed by record-breaking warm temperatures. Thawing snow left roads muddy and ditches filled with water. When Mom knew she was in actual labor, Doctor Lenarz instructed Dad to bring Mom by car to his house in Browerville. He would follow them the next fifteen miles to Bertha. Dad's dad accompanied them and word has it that Grandpa, in the backseat, prayed aloud as they approached two road graders, stuck side-by-side, on the muddy road. Dad shifted down, stepped on the accelerator, drove into the ditch filled with high water, around the graders, and out again. They journeyed on to meet Dr. Lenarz. Kenneth and Kevin waited to arrive until ten and fourteen minutes after reaching the hospital.

****

In 1946, Joseph was born in the Long Prairie Hospital. He lived six days. The hospital bill indicated forty-six dollars for his care that included a blood transfusion, administered directly from Lottie, the nurse, to Joseph. Joseph's condition was referred to as a blue baby, a heart condition. Mom was still in the hospital when Joseph was buried.

Len and I were the only siblings allowed at the graveside ceremony. Mom's sister was crying. She had lost several babies. In those days grieving mothers carried their pain alone. When Aunt Helen cried, I wondered why I didn't feel like crying. The vision of the little white, wooden casket remains with me. I wished I could have seen my baby brother, Joseph. I wished Mom and Dad could have held him. A couple of weeks later I saw tears running down Mom's cheeks as she guided unused blue baby clothes through the wringer of our Maytag washing machine. The clothes were packed away for future use.

By 1948, the Browerville Clinic, a long narrow brick building on a side street, was built for Dr. Lenarz and the community. Patients didn't make prior appoints, but simply went to the doctor's office, signed in and waited their turn. The waiting area usually had standing room only.

****

It was spring of my seventh grade at St. Peter's School. Ken, one of the twin brothers, then a second grader, was out for recess, running around the school. He collided with Louise, who had a clip in her hair that was dangling down her forehead. The accident resulted in both students receiving lacerations on or near their eyebrows. Sister Eymard, the principle of St. Peter's School and teacher of grades six, seven, and eight, summoned me and explained that I was to walk with the two younger students to Dr. Lenarz's office. Both students held cloths to their bleeding wounds. Both seemed calm for the four-block trek. I have no idea if the doctor or parents were notified.

At the clinic, the three of us were escorted to a back room, where the youngsters remained calm. I was thrilled to learn that I enjoyed watching Doctor Lenarz conduct the suturing process. On the farm, when veterinarians needed assistance, family members did what had to be done. Now I did what had to be done. With the procedures completed and bandages applied, we three students returned to school. I wondered if Doctor Lenarz and Sister Eymard were as proud of the two patients and me as I was.

In July 1948, my first sister was born, at the Long Prairie Hospital. Dad came home with the exciting news. I was nearly ten years old and finally, I had a sister after six brothers. She was named Jeanette Lucille. Kate arrived in September of 1949. A couple of special memories that come to mind of my sisters as toddlers: Jeanette and her daddy had an obvious special relationship. One evening Dad came in from the barn at dusk. Jeanette was already in her crib in our parent's bedroom for the night. One of her first clear sentences was; "Daddy, can't see." The family was in awe. Of, course, her dad went into the bedroom and picked her up. Kate weighed eleven pounds and five ounces at birth, and never looked like a newborn. She was the first and only sibling to have curly hair. Kate never crawled on all fours as most babies do. Her method of transportation was in a sitting position with her right foot tucked under her left knee. She, who usually wore dresses, scooted around the house and down steps causing callouses to form on her legs and the side of her right foot. She was a very self-sufficient little girl.

Charlie, a bit premature, arrived in November of 1950. Dad had given Mom a small brown suitcase as an early Christmas gift to be used for her pending trip to the hospital. It was stored in the closet of my upstairs bedroom. I had a sense something was wrong when Dad called upstairs for me to bring the gift downstairs six weeks early. It was Sunday morning. The guys were milking cows. Mom was dressed in her new, long green wool coat. As a daily routine Harold came shuffling into the house carrying a large kettle of milk at his knees. Usually someone older brought the milk from the barn to the house. This day flexibility was necessary. One side of the kettle slipped out of Harry's hand and warm milk spilled onto Mom's new coat. Mom took it in stride, dabbed and then washed off the milk while giving instructions as to who would ride with Grandpa Hoelscher to mass and who would stay home that day. I stayed home with younger children.

Grandpa Hoelscher wasn't exactly a safe driver, especially when he would go up Kline's hill in the left lane. We siblings held our breaths many a time when Grandpa's driving was questionable, yet I don't recall that he ever had an accident. Somebody up above was watching out for us. Special memories included Sundays after mass when Grandpa assigned one of us to take money from him and buy cherry jelly-filled deep fried bismarks from the Kuntz Bakery.

Later that Sunday, someone from Mom's family collected us and took us to pass the time at Grandma and Grandpa Becker's house, a mile away. In late afternoon, Grandma expressed concern that there had been no news from the hospital. Her comment was, "Lucille usually doesn't take this long." I was getting old enough to take on the concerns of others. Just before supper Dad came. Charlie, the preemie, took longer than full-term babies to do what had to be done. Fertility and birth intrigued me.

By late January, the baby was growing like a weed and all were healthy. Mom and Dad decided they wanted to give us an experience from their childhoods. It was a cold, clear, calm night. Dad took great pride in his team of horses. After milking the cows, the horses were harnessed and hooked up to a wooden wagon box on runners, with straw on the floor, and blankets to keep us warm.

Mom sat on a low stool with the baby swaddled in her arms. Dad standing with the reins in his hands masterfully commanded the horses across fields and through the woods to Grandpa and Grandma Becker's farm. We excited youngsters snuggled together to stay warm. Occasionally we would get to our knees to study the Norman Rockwell-type scenic view of the moon glistening on the snow. Fences were covered with snow. Dad guided the horses between fence posts.

Grandma and Grandpa may have thought their daughter and husband foolish for taking children on a sleigh ride in the cold of winter. Grandma made us hot chocolate and served her famous applesauce cake. I cherish that carefree event, one of the rare times that I felt like one of the gang, not the big sister. All of us kids experiencing something fun together for the first time.

Socially Challenged

****

If I, as a youngster, was excused from being Mother's right hand helper and wanted to play with siblings, I was expected to play boy's games. I did well for a girl, or so I was told. One day I complained to Mom that I never got to play girl's play. Mom ordered my brothers to play something that Millie enjoyed. We scrounged up clothes to play wedding and posed on the slanted cellar doors to the basement for a photo. One of the brothers wore a long flannel nightgown as a formal dress. There was a groom, a best man, a priest, and a flower girl. Another time we arranged furniture in the corn crib and a farm cat tolerated, maybe even enjoyed, being the baby in my doll buggy. Evening card games and playing hide and seek or steal sticks were fun group games. Often I was set apart from the brothers because Dad instructed them that I was to be treated with respect. They could tussle with each other but not me. Again, I was on the outside looking in.

It started out a warm-sunny March day. Some students wore winter coats to school. I donned a long, belted, yellow plaid coat that was Aunt Barb's, Mom's younger sister. By mid-day the wind was picking up with snow flying. We were instructed to get our coats and boots on. The buses would pick us up shortly. Our bus got stuck out in the country. Farmers came with tractors to pull us out. The bus driver decided to turn back and get over to the main road that ran by Mom's parent's house. My aunt and uncle were dropped off at their house.

Millie Hoelscher Moran

Linus and I continued on to the next intersection. The driver decided he could not take the chance of driving on the side road so he left the two of us off to fend for ourselves over a hill and more than a half-mile facing into the wind. The sun was still shining, temperatures were dropping and wind blowing the snow into our faces. Prior to the top of the hill, we did okay. Once over the hill and facing west, I crouched down every so often, turning my back to the wind and covering the long coat over my bare legs. Linus refused to put on his mittens or lower his ear flaps.

Thanks to the telephone party-line our parents were aware of the bus turning around, though didn't know what had happened to their children. Likely Grandma let them know that we did not get off the bus at their house. Dad met us at the end of our driveway with blankets. I was a fair distance behind Linus, who told Dad to take the blankets to me. Once home I realized I came through the experience pretty well. Len had frozen his ears and thumbs.

My class numbers at St. Peter's fluctuated between eight to ten students depending on the year. Many Catholic country students attended small one-room country schools. The year farm children made their Solemn Communion some parents would make arrangements for children to attend that one year at the Catholic school. Prior to bussing, a few of our neighbors carpooled so I attended St. Peter's School all eight years. The other three girls in my class all lived in town. Country kids were like second-class citizens.

Socially Challenged

Students from town hung together all year long. Country kids went home after school to assist with farm and house chores.

****

When I got to the upper grades, I started to slowly come out of my self-inflicted protective shell. I was quite good at games played in school when it was too cold or rainy to go outside and sports activities on suitable weather days. On Valentine's Day, I received a valentine from Chuck, who sat across the aisle from me. It was likely a previously used card, not the typical kid's cards. A name had been erased from the bottom. It had a folded-down flower stem that when pulled up read; "I hope your love for me will grow and grow and grow." When I looked over at Chuck he was watching me read. Maybe I smiled. Maybe not.

Our school was at the top of a hill and sledding conditions down the side street through several intersections were excellent; dangerous, but excellent. I got brave enough to climb on a sled with a boy classmate. It was exhilarating, almost flying through the fresh air, literally. At about the same time, the school held a paper drive. We were given an extended lunch hour for seventh and eighth graders to venture all over town with sleds collecting boxed or tied newspapers. This was more boy/girl time. I was beginning to wish that I lived in town. When I got back to the classroom, I had blood on my leg, no pain, just blood. Sister accompanied me out of the room with a puzzled look on her face. I simply needed a Band Aid, probably nicked my shin on a sled.

In family life I had been conditioned as a detective to report questionable sibling behavior to Mom, who explained that she couldn't have eyes and ears everywhere. I hated the responsibility but believed it a parental order so took it seriously. On some occasions when I reported my version of behaviors to Mom, she would pass it on to Dad. A few times this resulted in beatings that left me regretting reporting my version of an incident and made me want to run away from home. How could my siblings view me as an equal or respect me?

Once, I told Mom about an incident in school of something like a white balloon, but not a balloon, being passed among eighth graders and guilty-type giggling taking place. Mom told me to tell Sister, who advised me that if it happened again to write on a piece of paper "So and So has it." The white balloon-type object never again appeared. A few days later on the playground I asked Charlotte what that was. She replied; "I just went to Confession about that day and I don't want to talk about it." By that time I had a pretty good idea what "it" was.

The spring before graduating from St. Peter's School in Browerville, my brother Allen was born. I stayed home from school a few days to assist the family. We had hired help, as well. A few months later, Mom had most of her teeth removed and was fitted with dentures. Dentures were common in those days, though it was believed that pregnancy depleted the mother's body of calcium. The house was remodeled that summer to accommodate the growing family. The kitchen became a laundry room plus provided for a cabinet for farm clothes, toys and utility supplies. A huge dining room became a kitchen. The porch was enclosed and served as a multi-purpose room. Finally, we had an indoor bathroom, with a bathtub, but no shower.

One hot August day; 1952, I was hanging clothes on the line to the west of the house when the public school superintendent drove into the yard to talk primarily to my parents and then a few words with me about starting grade nine in the fall. Mom and Dad said it was my decision though the many perils of public school had been engrained in me. I was apprehensive about leaving the Catholic setting though my biggest concern was that I hadn't begun to menstruate as yet.

I bargained with God: "If the onset of menstruation happened before the start of the first day of school I would ask to go to town and purchase school supplies and a few new clothes." Mom had talked to me about menstruation and what I might expect. Still I decided I wanted to be experienced in coping with this rite of passage before facing the unknowns of the outside world. How I longed for peer girlfriends or older sisters to clue me in on the subject from a teen perspective, though Mom cautioned that this was a topic to discuss only with her.

The bus picked up my siblings that first day of school and I slept in late. In1952, the majority of students in the area attended high school. Several young people, myself included, stayed home to assist with family and/or farm labor. At the time the compulsory Federal Child Labor and Education Laws required parents to provide children with formal education until age fourteen. That law changed to age sixteen in 1954.

****

I crawled out of bed Tuesday morning, November 4, 1952, wearing red and white hand-me-down pajamas. The warm wet sensation between my thighs sent me charging down the stairs as I gestured, asking Mom; "Is this what you meant?" She whisked me off to her bedroom for her version of feminine supplies, a four-by-seven inch thinned flannel diaper folded several times and quilted. She instructed me to pin the pad inside of my undergarments. Remnants of sheets, towels, aprons and so on were laid on the pad and replaced throughout the day as necessary.

Next Mom brought out a small pink booklet regarding girls and sexuality that she read to me. I asked her; "If girls bleed, what do boys do?" She confidently explained that in their teens or as young adults, males may or may not have wet dreams (nocturnal emissions) and I might sometimes see whitish-yellowish spots on my brother's bed sheets. If I noticed such stains I should report it to her. Mom went on to explain that all of this was normal and part of God's Plan. She showed me the blue booklet that she had for the boys, but I didn't get to read it. President Eisenhower was elected that day. I never noticed evidence of a discharge on my brother's sheets, either.

Had I started ninth grade I likely would have dropped out within a few weeks. Mom, fatigued from all of the stress she encountered that summer, suffered physical and emotional exhaustion. She required hospitalization in St. Paul. The oldest child personality in me stepped up and I became "the mom" for months to come.

For my fourteenth birthday I received a wristwatch from my parents. I believed it was because I stayed home from high school and worked so hard to keep the family running smoothly while Mom was ill. Then Dad sold a calf and half of the money was divided amongst the six oldest children (the first family). I was dumbfounded when I, the oldest, and hardworking in my eyes, received a dollar amount. Len and Harry received more than me. The three younger boys received less than me. I sensed Dad valued man's work more than women's work. That evening I sulked.

When Mom stabilized and throughout my teen years I worked for a few dollars a day to help relatives and neighbors when a new baby arrived in their families. The next year Len ended his formal education after eighth grade, as well. I felt derailed when he also received a wristwatch for his fourteenth birthday. It became a tradition. It was no longer an award for staying home from school to assist the parents and growing family.

By age fifteen I was selected to be godmother to newborn Gerard. Mom and Dad's parents and most of their siblings already held the godparent honor with my previous siblings. Gerard must have fit right in with the rest of the family. He was one of many in which I played a significant part in their learning to walk, talk and be potty trained. That must have been a relatively calm time in the family. I remember so little of the events surrounding Ger's toddler years. One time was when Mom informed this cowboy of a little man that he sometimes needed to play girl's games with his sister. I had to smile when I walked into the playroom and Gerard was making a galloping horse sound as he held a miniature toy horse and rider galloping on the roof of the girl's dollhouse.

My younger siblings were getting old enough to assist with house and farm responsibilities. Life was growing calmer, for a few months or maybe years.

As a teenager, feeling isolated in adult responsibilities, fantasizing swept me away to visions of a life beyond the farm. Few girls went to college. If they did it was to acquire nursing, teaching or secretarial skills. Some would work as store clerks or waitresses. A few pursued training to become airline stewardesses. I was going through a period of discerning whether I felt drawn to a life of marriage or as a nun. Mostly, I longed for an education.

One Saturday forenoon, with most of the family mulling around the house, I took a comic book from the buffet drawer on the porch and went from one age-appropriate family member to another and asked them to guess if there were more words beginning with an *M* or *S* on the page. I wrote their responses at the top of the page, one letter per page. I acted alone and with little interruption of their conversations. If more *M*s I would lean toward marriage, if *S*s I would consider becoming a nun more seriously. One family member declined to participate and the outcome was a tie.

Chapter Two

By 1955, the weekly issue of the *Browerville Blade* was printing articles and notices of meetings intended to rally support for a Catholic hospital to be built in Browerville. Some residents questioned the wisdom for doing so in this community with a population of 635 people. Most were excited. Doctor Lenarz emphasized that area hospitals were small and outdated. He believed the timing was right to build a Catholic healthcare facility in our primarily Catholic community.

The sketched architectural plans indicated that the facility would offer thirty-two patient beds, notably larger than surrounding rural hospitals. The structure would offer two private rooms, a pediatric room with four cribs and the rest would be double rooms. While not as elaborate as the St. Cloud Hospital, St. Gabriel's in Little Falls or St. Joseph's in Brainerd, Browerville people rose to the occasion and supported the plan. Along with improved and available healthcare, a new hospital would provide employment to area residents. The Benedictine Sisters from Crookston signed on to staff leadership positions. Father Columban, a Benedictine priest, was assigned as hospital chaplain. St. John's was the name given to Browerville's hospital.

I was seventeen years old when the hospital neared completion. In the spring of 1956, when my cohorts were finishing their senior year of high school, I joined area residents in painting hospital rooms in preparation for open house day. Next I applied for a nurse's aide position and volunteered as a tour guide for open house day. When pointing out a utility room, a gentleman asked me; "What are those metal containers on the counter used for?" I guessed and responded; "Measuring." At the time I didn't know it was a urinal.

A week later I was called to the hospital for a job interview. I remember little about the interview other than it was informal. I told the interviewing nun that I had promised my aunt and uncle I would help them out when their baby arrived and that I would need a month off in July when my mother's baby was due.

My cousin, Tim, was the first baby born at the St. John's. I was caring for him and his family when the call came from Sister Paula, asking me to start work as soon as possible. I requested a few extra days to allow me to complete my commitment to the new parents and to shop for a uniform. Nurse's shoes and fabric to sew an additional uniform would have to wait until after my first check. My pay, forty cents an hour, paid every two weeks, meant it would be awhile before I'd have comfortable shoes. My first day of employment was March 19, 1956, the feast of St. Joseph, patron of workers. Although exhausted at the end of each day, I felt blessed. Doors to a bigger world were opening to me.

Sister Jacquelyn taught me how to give bed baths and change beds with patients in them. We nurse's aides were taught the daily schedule for meals, baths, taking vitals certain times a day, ambulating patients and cleaning beds of discharged patients. Each morning our patient assignments were found on the schedule posted in the diet kitchen. The boxed, no-window kitchenette had limited supplies for patients and staff. Patient water pitchers, small drinking glasses and trays filled the limited cabinet space. The refrigerator kept penicillin cooled. A two-burner electric hot plate, a table with two chairs and a bulletin board completed the furnishings of the room which served a valuable purpose.

Giving enemas and prepping patients for surgery were added to aide's routines. About a month into the job, Sister slowly introduced me to the nursery. I felt privileged and wondered if being chosen for this job had something to do with my experience in a large family. Mixing Similac formula was added to my responsibilities. Taking babies to their mothers to be fed during the daytime was the practice. Formula was taken to mothers even if they were breastfeeding. Society was going through a phase of assuming a woman could not produce enough milk. A few experienced lactating mothers refused the formula.

As months passed I was taught to transfer newborns from the incubator in the delivery room and admit them to the nursery. Cleaning, weighing and measuring the infant with a tape measure held to the heels and lifting the heels upward with the dangling baby stretched was considered the most accurate way to measure length of a healthy newborn. Baby was dressed and bundled to keep warm. One silver nitrate drop was squeezed into each eye of the sleepy newborn. I didn't question the reason for the drops, I simply did as I was told. Years later I learned the silver nitrate was to prevent sexually transmitted infection that could be contracted from the mother when passing through the birth canal. The common belief was that this infection could cause blindness in the child. Documenting pertinent information gradually became familiar to me. Then it was time to introduce the newborn to its mother.

July 2, 1956, Mom was admitted to the hospital as a patient in labor. I was able to spend time with her in the labor room before heading home to prepare lunch for the family. The mother-daughter time allowed for me to get an empathetic sense of discomfort during labor. Mom was a trooper. Greg was born a few hours later. For her own reasons, Mom chose to breastfeed every other child. Greg was bottle-fed. Actually, even her breastfed babies received supplemental bottles. I learned decades later that supplemental feedings can lead to an earlier return of fertility. Supposedly, the baby's sucking supresses ovulation, and that could explain why Mom became pregnant so soon after every birth. Only the twins were born less than a year apart. I took a one-month maternity leave, as agreed upon when hired. Apparently the family got through the summer easily—I don't remember much of that summer.

Husbands rarely remained at the hospital while the wife was in labor and delivery. Most men would carry in a wife's luggage and walk with her to the admissions desk, where she was turned over to a nurse to be escorted to the labor room. Once I witnessed a husband stopping the car out in the street and the wife got out, with suitcase in hand, to fend for herself. She walked up the sidewalk and checked herself in.

Men would leave for several hours to do who knows what. Rumor had it that the town liquor store was a common hangout for fathers-in-waiting. After returning to the hospital to get the news of the wife's condition and the sex of the baby, a small town ritual was that the father would purchase "It's a boy" or "It's a girl" banded cigars to hand out to other men.

Uncle Glen, as was the practice, dropped off his wife, who was taken to the labor room. Labor was short and when Uncle Glen returned to the hospital, Sister Paula from the front business office asked if I would escort him to his wife in the labor room. The hospital was filled to capacity and the new obstetrical patient was being held in the labor room until a bed opened up on the floor following a patient discharge.

Uncle Glen was asking his wife how she was doing and it became apparent that we all thought others had told him that he had a son. He appeared stunned upon hearing the news and I asked if he would like to go with me to the adjacent and only delivery room that was empty except for soiled sheets, instruments, placenta in a container on the floor and the incubator with the newborn enclosed. He followed me and we stood in silence and gazed upon the chunky newest cousin covered with the white vernix. At the time I couldn't describe how I felt. As I developed spiritually I realized it was a God moment. Uncle Glen and I spent time in silence. I wondered what he was thinking.

One wing of the hospital consisting of ten beds was reserved for surgical and obstetrical patients. My assigned patients were generally from this group. Every day was a new experience. I thrived on the knowledge and stimulation. Contrary to the medical wing, most of my patients were on the mend and would soon be discharged. It was an upbeat job. Hospital stays for OB patients were three or four days, cesarean births could be a week. Surgical patients might stay up to a week or ten days depending on the procedure. Bonding with patients was a happy time.

Observing the RNs was how I was prepared to monitor post-operative patients. I was always in the mindset of, "If you think I can do this, I can do it." Nurse's aides were conditioned to do what was asked of us though we didn't always know the reason for doing what we did. Higher-level patient care went on around us and we could easily be oblivious to the whys and wherefores. Sometimes we might figure something out but I operated on somewhat of a "don't ask . . . don't tell" basis. I assumed there was a reason for certain approaches to patient care and confidentiality was

Millie Hoelscher Moran

paramount. I suspect that I functioned as a zombie and often was amazed at how I was capable of doing more than I dreamed for myself. It wasn't highschool and it wasn't college . . . it was on-the-job training.

Chapter Three

As responsibilities maneuvered me throughout the large addition to Browerville, second only in size and employees to the Browerville Milk Plant, I became aware that crucifixes hung on walls in all rooms of this medical facility except linen closets, utility rooms and restrooms. Statues of saints were strategically placed in waiting rooms, staircase landings or ends of corridors. These artifacts added to the ambiance of being on holy ground. While reassuring patients and visitors, these visuals were reminders to employees as well.

    Janet had graduated from nurse's training at the St. Cloud Hospital. I knew she graduated from the Browerville High School and I was aware of some of her relatives though Janet and I first met at St. John's. Her nurse's cap and pin on her white uniform dress, the white nylon hose and white shoes won my admiration. She had a pleasant, calm personality. Our relationship was strictly a work relationship. About a week after starting at the hospital Janet asked me to join her in helping her turn an eighty-nine-year-old dying male patient so she could take his temperature rectally. The only male bodies I had seen in my life was when changing diapers or bathing preschoolers. As Janet inserted the rectal thermometer, I was tempted to quit this job. After swallowing a few times it hit me ... "If Janet can do something that seemed so distasteful, I would do whatever was asked of me in this hospital setting." I was determined to be the best compassionate patient care person I could be.

Observing Janet as being part of the 7:00 a.m. report, making rounds with doctors, returning from the operating room in her scrubs, setting up and passing meds or updating patient's charts with a quiet demeanor calmed my jitters as I aimed to function in an environment which I realized was totally out of my league. I felt privileged if she invited me to go to lunch with her. Perhaps she lunched with other aides too. I don't remember.

Janet's brother had returned to the area following his tour of duty with the United States Navy. He had minor surgery. I was assigned to take his vitals as the anesthetic was wearing off. Dan repeatedly proclaimed that he had to go to the head. I had never heard that term before though assumed that it was navy jargon for restroom. This was never discussed with Janet, another co-worker or anyone else for that matter. Head was another new vocabulary word that rang in my mind for a few days.

This idolized nurse was dating an out-of-town man. One morning as I was giving a surgical patient a bed bath Janet came into the room to the opposite side of the bed and placed both of her hands on the patient, as if to be holding the person in place for me. I silently questioned the gesture and wondered if she was ordered to observe me. We left the room and Janet informed me that she and Ben became engaged over the weekend. A light bulb went on. Her engagement ring was on her left hand holding the patient and I was so wrapped up in giving a good job performance that I totally missed the ring. I was embarrassed. I was invited to and attended the wedding a few months later, a cold winter Minnesota day. The bride had laryngitis. Janet continued working and took maternity leave when her first baby was born.

About that time Sister Jacquelyn informed me that I would have on-the-job training for being the circling nurse in surgery. Both Sister and Janet gently guided me through maneuvers that are vague. One of the first items emphasized on the learning list was counting bloody four-by-four or four-by-eight inch gauze sponges. It was as if I was numb and learning through osmosis. I suspect those women, and probably doctors, too, were praying for me. I was praying for my performance and the patient's welfare, always with a fear of what damage I might innocently cause. I asked few questions and sometimes when I did laughter erupted like the day I was prepping a patient for a mastectomy, which included shaving a large area around the breast including the axilla. I meekly went to the nurse's station where two RNs were charting and asked, "While shaving the patient should I shave both armpits?" The laughter haunted me. I forged on and decided that if I were the patient I would want both underarms shaved. So I did exactly that.

Chapter Four

Attending community sporting events and dancing at dance halls in communities surrounding Browerville was a primary source of mingling with peers. Thanks to aunts and uncles, I was also introduced to the Medina Lanes Ballroom in a Minneapolis suburb. I dated occasionally and exchanged letters with friends serving in the military, no serious relationships. This nursing job was introducing me to male patients my age or a few years older. While there was never any flirting that I was aware of, on occasion I struggled with taking a professional route and sometimes I failed.

One of the rare times I worked a three o'clock to eleven o'clock shift, Luke, a few years my senior and someone that I had a crush on, was admitted for next day surgery. I was the admitting nurse. He was given his hospital gown and left to undress, hang his clothes in the closet and crawl in bed. I returned with a pitcher of water, a thermometer, a blood pressure cuff and the scales to weigh him. I noticed that he had tied his gown in front rather than the back. I didn't have the heart to tell him. I was hoping Luke would notice how his roommate had his gown tied in the back. He got out of bed as directed and climbed on the scale. I left to admit the next patient but was stopped by the supervising night nurse and reprimanded for not having the patient reverse the gown. I wondered if the nun had ever felt self-conscious with a scantily-clad young male patient looking her in the eyes.

Eighteen-year-old Ralph had fractured his back and was confined to six weeks of lying on his back in a room in the medical wing of the hospital, so I rarely went to his room. After work one day I decided to visit my grandpa, who was a patient across the hall from Ralph. On my way out I floated into Ralph's room to chat a bit. There on his nightstand was a *Playboy* magazine. That magazine was unacceptable in my world. I nonchalantly, without comment, picked up the sexy periodical, bid farewell, and headed to the hospital incinerator. I can't believe that I actually admit to this.

Another fellow whose name I can't recall was a short-term patient. As instructed, I went to his room to prepare him for discharge. I got his clothes from the closet and asked him if he had underwear. No underwear! Oh my gosh! Wearing blue jeans without briefs was new to me. I managed to not react outwardly. I was maturing.

There was this older gentleman who was on strict bed rest, which meant no getting out of bed. We nurses were trained to give patients bed baths and then offer them a washcloth and towel to finish their bath (their private parts) while the nurse left the room to refill the water pitcher with fresh water. When I returned, the patient had gotten up out of bed, crossed the room and was bent over the sink washing his baldhead. I reported the incident to the supervisor. We remained somber. I was reminded of Arthur Godfrey, radio/television entertainer of the fifties who said; "Nurses tell patients that they will wash the patient as far down as possible and as far up as possible and then will leave the room while the patient washes possible."

Again, I didn't express my feelings, this time anger. A nineteen-year-old guy that I didn't know was asleep on the operating table having surgery for an umbilical hernia repair. The surgeon had closed the incision and at the last minute when suturing the skin back in place he announced that he wasn't going to deal with the belly button and snipped it off. We were informed that the patient didn't need a belly button anyway. I was furious but held in my thoughts of wondering if no belly button would be traumatic for the patient. My blood still boils when I think about that decision. Maybe it didn't bother the patient. I will never know.

Rick was a tall, handsome guy. We rode the school bus together when I was in eighth grade and he in tenth. When he'd get on the bus my stomach fluttered and I wondered how I would act if he would sit in the seat next to me. He always sat with another girl. After high school he went into the military and was serving in Korea when his father, John, had surgery. I was circulating in the operating room during the procedure, though never gathered from the surgeon's and scrub nurses' conversations that implied this was a case of advanced cancer.

John was my patient following surgery. After a few days I was instructed to sit him up in the chair in his room in preparation for the arrival of his son who was called home from Korea on a medical discharge to take over the farm. I stepped out of the room and choked up as the two embraced. John succumbed to cancer a few months later. Rick married another woman.

Chapter Five

My paternal grandmother was diagnosed with leukemia in December of 1942, and died a few weeks later. In the forties and fifties cancer was being diagnosed more frequently. Cancer might have been referred to as "that dreaded disease" or the "C word." If a person was diagnosed with the generally incurable condition, the doctor or family members might decide not to tell the patient. Most were concerned that the disease was contagious. I was among that frightened group.

Mrs. Justin had surgery and was released from the hospital. She returned often for a few days each time appearing to have lost more weight. Finally she was nearing the end of life with her family at her bedside. Candles were lit and a crucifix sat on the nightstand. I had absolutely no experience with the dying process. Leslie, another nurse's aide, and I followed orders to ask the family to step out of the room while we freshened up Mrs. Justin's bed. I knew the doctor and registered nurses were already scrubbing for a scheduled surgery. As gently as possible we turned the patient on her back. Her eyes opened wide and her gaze and hands reached for the ceiling. With an unimaginable strength she raised her upper body to an almost sitting position. Then she laid back and her head to the left toward me. A dark brown liquid ran from her mouth.

I panicked and ran out of the room thinking, "I am not prepared for this." Leslie, the other aide, seemed to remain calm and stayed with the patient. I dashed by the family and headed to OR and informed the doctor that I thought Mrs. Justin had died. Doctor removed his gloves and went to the patient's room and talked with the family. For me it was more on-the-job training. Thank God for Leslie!

Another cancer patient was an older man, by my standards at that time, tall and slender with a laryngectomy, which meant he couldn't talk and was fed through an opening at the base of his neck. I was afraid of him and one day was assigned to bathe him. Alone with him in the room, he proceeded to crawl out of bed. The faster I moved toward the door . . . the faster he moved after me and trying to clutch me. I managed to get my foot between the door and the frame. He was pushing the door closed and I pulled it open and dashed down the hall looking for someone to rescue me. When no one could be found the patient set his near-bare body down on the tile floor. Often I could have used a sounding board to help me work through some of these frightening situations. I never brought up subjects to supervisors and for confidentially reasons couldn't bring it up at home. This time however, I boldly informed Sister Jacquelyn that I would never again enter that man's room alone.

Mr. Parker, on the other hand, was a very gentle person who also had cancer. He was in room 104 bed A. As his condition worsened and he could no longer walk down the hall to the restroom a commode was positioned at his bedside. I remember emptying the commode containing a very dark liquid. My stomach tightened and my heart ached for this man and his large family. I wondered if cancer was contagious. One morning I got to work and his bed had been stripped.

Fatigue began to plague me. I was dropping things. Twice I was taking patient temperatures and I dropped the rack containing a dozen or more thermometers. Most of the thermometers broke. What a mess. I apologized and wasn't asked to pay for them. I don't remember who suggested that I have a blood test because I wasn't my normal self. A complete blood count was ordered and my hemoglobin count was seven. My doctor ordered me to be admitted to the hospital immediately and I was assigned to room 104a. (Oh dread!) I didn't advocate for myself, but moving into Mr. Parker's bed weighed heavily on my spirit. A week of tests, x-rays and two blood transfusions and other IV nutrients put me in a position to experience what it was like being on the receiving end of patient care. Much of the experience was a blur. One day I got permission to take my meal tray to the room of another nurse's aide who was a patient at the opposite end of the hospital. I dropped the tray. Food and broken dishes flew everywhere. I expected to be reprimanded or have to pay for the damage. Again, no one said anything to me.

After being discharged I returned to my doctor for a routine follow-up visit. He posed the question: "Mildred, usually it is parents that get ulcers from worrying about their children, is there something going on between you and you parents?" He knew our family situation. I said very little though realized I could have used a counselor or mentor to accompany me as I tried to imagine myself transitioning from life on the farm to a life out in the world without a high school or college education. In addition I thoroughly enjoyed the opportunity to work in surgery, though responsibilities given to me that I deemed way beyond my training caused stress. I feared for the patient's welfare. I again tried to convince myself that if my supervisors gave me the job and I wasn't fired, just give it my best, and I did.

As an oldest child in the large family followed by six brothers, my position in the family was like limbo. I had little in common with my brothers. Society at that time dictated that children were to be seen and not heard. So questions to adults were kept to a minimum. I had aunts and uncles close to my age but my status in the family was lower than theirs. I always felt like I was on the outside looking in and not as an equal. At the hospital it felt the same. Nurse's aides were never part of report at the beginning or end of a shift. So often I felt that if I was better informed I would be less stressed.

Millie Hoelscher Moran

In addition, I was the only aide working in surgery, so consequently I spent little time with other aides and most of the daytime shift people were older than me. In all situations I felt like I was on the outside looking in longing for emotional support. However, I believed I was in the right place at the time, especially when patients greeted me with; "Good morning, Sunshine!" as they awaited their baths or showers.

By this time my peers had moved on to college, military or jobs outside of Browerville. I willingly worked overtime at the hospital, all for forty cents an hour. I never asked for more. Sometimes Sister Mary Paul would ask me if I was okay with being given a five dollar meal coupon booklet for ten meals rather than payment for overtime. Whether that was a plus or a minus I don't know. All I knew was that the hospital proved to be the most desirable place I could imagine working until I was shown another respectable path. I prayed for guidance and continued to grow in wisdom, understanding, fortitude, knowledge and perhaps other things. My experiences were preparing me for unknowns.

Chapter Six

Entering Browerville in the 1950s, travelers from both the north and south on US Highway 71 could spot a road sign which read: "BROWERVILLE pop. 635." Granted, the farms outside of town were likely to have houses and gardens that accommodated and fed the large families that operated the farms. One or two tiny churches were out in the country though the community itself had one Lutheran church with a pastor and two Catholic Churches. Saint Joseph's Church served the Polish population and St. Peter's Church nurtured the German families. Each Catholic Church had its own pastor, a school with grades one to eight and all teachers were Benedictine Sisters from St. Benedict's in St. Joseph, Minnesota.

The new Catholic Hospital's leadership staff was from Crookston, Minnesota. Father Columban, a Benedictine priest, arrived to provide spiritual care as the hospital chaplain. Every morning at six a.m., mass was celebrated in the hospital chapel, mostly for the sisters. Occasionally a patient or family member might participate. Hospital staff sometimes attended as well. I did on Sundays when I worked 7:00 a.m. to 3:30p.m. or I would take a lunch break to attend mass with my faith congregation and then work later into the afternoon. When passing by the chapel during the workday a quick visit to the Blessed Sacrament offered me reassurance and confidence as I accepted challenges that left me with feelings that were to difficult to tell to others. Jesus was my confidant and counselor.

Daily, the eleven to seven nursing staff would prepare patients desiring to receive communion in their rooms by straightening beds, raising the head of the bed, offering the patient a washcloth and comb or brush if requested to get prepared for the solemn start to their day. One of the sisters, usually one wearing a long white habit, carried a lit candle and preceded Father Columban for this ritual. Shortly thereafter patients would have their lab testing, get their breakfast trays, be taken downstairs for x-rays or whisked off to surgery. Then the daily patient care process of baths, hygiene and walking or up to a chair as ordered ensued. Hopefully there were not too many discharges leaving beds to be cleaned.

Father Columban also administered the Sacrament of Extreme Unction to the near-death patients. The Sacraments of Penance to those requesting it and Baptism to frail infants were Father's responsibility. I was asked to be a proxy sponsor for three babies, all boys. Two of the babies survived. I visited both for several years after. One was likely a cerebral palsy baby and the other was the product of parents with the RH incompatibility problem. This little guy required several blood exchanges and one day when no RNs or LPNs other than Sister Jacquelyn were working I was charged with scrubbing in for the procedure. Sister guided me through my first scrub and to assist the doctor in doing the exchange process.

    The doctor would withdraw a few cc of blood from the baby's umbilical cord, redirect that blood to a container on the floor, draw in a few cc of blood from the fresh unit hanging from a standard and plunge the blood through the syringe into the baby's umbilical cord. This was repeated many times for the exchange and if necessary again at a future date until the billirubin count stabilized. This was one of those God moments. Not only was I instrumental in this lifesaving event, I was being prepared for my own life and my babies that would require blood exchanges. What a blessing!

    A preemie born at six months gestation was baptized. He required gavage feedings. A couple of we nurse's aides were taught to gavage feed by injecting a few cc of formula from a syringe into a tube inserted up his nose and down his throat into the stomach of the baby in the incubator. Family members were not allowed into the nursery. (The adorable little dark curly haired girl who could barely peek over the bottom of the nursery window in an effort to see her brother would one day become my sister-in-law.) One morning I got to work and the incubator was empty. It was a day of grief for me.

Millie Hoelscher Moran

Another relative in her forties was brought into the hospital hemorrhaging profusely. She thought she was about six months pregnant. The patient was rushed into OR for emergency surgery. The anesthetic was given. Doctors and nurses were scrubbing and I was instructed how to do my first bladder catheterization before assisting the docs and the nurse in gowning. Blood was in the urine. The gift of calm in an emergency is unexplainable other than it is simply a grace-filled moment.

The abdominal incision was made. In coaching me, Sister told me that there may or may not be a baby found in the mother's uterus, but if there was a baby I was to take it outside the OR and baptize it. There was a lifeless tiny baby boy that was handed to me. I took him to the scrub sinks and baptized him three times to make sure I did it right. (So much for "calm.") Pro-life and abortion weren't issues in the fifties but now there was no doubt for me. This little one resembled his brothers. I saw life as never before. This dead, stillborn cousin profoundly impacted me forever. I heard later that Fr. Columban supposedly repeated the ritualistic conditional baptism. The mother's life was saved.

As a farm girl I much preferred to drive the green family Plymouth to work. Occasionally I was instructed to take the half-ton pickup used on the farm as my transportation. When I did I would take the back streets into town to the hospital. One day after work I hopped into the Ford pickup, prepared for a quick escape out of town, when Fr. Columban stopped me and for the first time ever, asked me for a ride downtown. How could I refuse? He asked to be dropped off in the center of town in front of the Liquor Store. Mortification! I wondered if these Benedictines were in cahoots with my mother, trying to find out what I was made of. Mom prayed for many of her children to become priests or sisters. She probably even expressed her wishes to her Benedictine buddies.

Chapter Seven

Two young children left a permanent stamp on my heart. Both were from out of the area. An out-of-town doctor brought an obstetrical patient to St. John's to deliver her baby. I was instructed to take the mother's belongings from the labor room to room 115, a two-bed room, which I did. The patient in the far bed asked who her new roommate was going to be. I read the name on the luggage and got an ear full. I listened; and controlled my reactions. I was informed that the woman had several children and that her husband died in a train accident about a year earlier. The woman suggested that there must be some mistake.

The next thing I knew I was instructed to change the new mother's room to a single room at the far opposite end of the hospital. She had an awful cold and the baby would not be taken to the mother. This was one of those awkward times. With all newborns, my job was to take the baby's footprints and the mother's thumbprints for the birth certificate. I was also to give the traditional formula, Dreft detergent and other items as a gift pack to the new mothers. I did the prints but just could not get myself to take the gift pack to the mother. I left it on the counter at the back of the nurse's station. I anticipated that someone else would make the decision or question me about it. No one did.

One day when Sr. Jacquelyn and I were transporting a sleeping patient on a gurney from the operating room to the patient's room, I closed the door behind us and informed Sr. Jacquelyn that; "We have to talk!" I was slowly growing more assertive. I felt compelled to let Sister know how awkward all of this was for me.

Shortly thereafter the mother was discharged. The beautiful black haired, round-faced darling baby remained for several weeks. The staffpeople fed him, often propping a bottle of formula while attending to other nursery tasks, we'd burp, bathe, weigh, change the diaper and turn the little guy. His feet were always so cold that we put a warm water pack at the bottom of the basinet. One day I noticed his feet were peeling. Apparently one of us, possibly me, had the water temperature to hot in the rubber water bottle and it burned the baby's feet. My heart ached.

Eventually Sr. Jacquelyn informed me that I was to prepare formula to go with the baby when the social worker would come before the morning shift to take the infant somewhere. Every time my mother had a baby, new clothes were purchased for go home day. For this no name baby there was a small stack of clean, used, unmatched baby clothes on the counter in the formula room, waiting for the discharge of this little bundle. My stomach tightened, and a tear rolled down my cheek. I prayed that this little angel would know happiness in his life. I still pray for him.

On another occasion a two-year-old girl had been admitted since my last workday. I didn't recognize her name. The cardex file had little information and I considered charts as RN and LPN responsibilities. I was told the little one was the youngest in a large family. She was in a pediatric crib, alone in the room. She took milk in a bottle but little food. She seemed to have a normal temperature and outwardly healthy but emotionally distant and unreachable. I remember Janet, the RN, sitting with the child and offering her soft foods.

I'm assuming, but maybe wrong, that people I thought were her parents visited the hospital. The door to the child's room was left ajar so they could look at the child without letting the child see them. It wasn't adding up. I asked no questions. As with young siblings that I enjoyed interacting with, I took it upon myself to spend some time in the little girl's room and try to get her to smile. Patient numbers were down and I had time to carry her out into the hall near the nurse's station and the nursery. No one stopped me or made any comments. I've often wondered what the story was behind this situation. I was beginning to get the sense that we, as hospital staff, cared for patient's physical needs, but in the fifties I wondered what happened with psychological needs. I wondered if she was going to be placed in a foster home.

Occasionally nurse's aides would be summoned to work together to clean up a person from heaven only knew where. We worked together respectfully as a team, no giggling or comments. Within a day or so the patient was gone.

It was a beautiful summer day. A middle-aged man was brought in and deposited in a private room. We aides were at a loss as to where and how to begin. The stench left no doubt that a bath, shampoo, and a shave would be necessary. With a hospital gown and robe handy the peeling off of clothing began. On this warm summer day, the fellow was wearing long wool winter underwear. He disclosed that he changed his underwear once a year when he took a bath at Easter time. Sister Jacquelyn had given me a poem early on in my employment with the words; "Oh Christian nurse, remember that men are more than things." This man of God was taken to a bathtub to soak. I remember the grimy ring in the bathtub and then was called away to assist with something else. That was the last I saw of this gentleman.

On another occasion a woman was brought in and again the assignment to we aides was that she needed to be cleaned up. Again, the perplexed gazes of we white uniformed aides: Where to begin? It was decided that the woman's slightly graying hair required shampooing. It must have been years since a brush made it through her hair, that was more like a thick gnarled nest. The hair was solidly entangled into a roll on the back of her head. Shampooing alone would not suffice. Our team agreed that the roll had to be cut out. I owned a bandage scissors so retrieved it from my pocket. I can still hear the crunch-crunch sound as I cut into the collection of grains of sand. It wasn't pretty. I wondered what the woman was thinking. I don't remember asking her. We were following directions. I was thinking: "But for the grace of God, there go I."

Andrew and his brother apparently lived alone. The only reason I remember his name is because he must have remained with us for about a year. Upon arrival his muscles and tendons were ridged. He was stooped and needed assistance walking. He rarely spoke, though was able to feed himself and seemed to enjoy eating. The hospital staff met his bodily needs of cleaning and feeding. Engaging him in conversation was beyond my ability, though I tried. His brother visited him about once a month. Andrew developed gangrene on his foot and he was taken to surgery. His leg was amputated at the knee. I cleaned up the operating room and instruments after surgery. That lower leg and foot lying on the counter in the surgery utility room was another snippet to be added to my memory bank.

In caring for Andrew in the days following surgery I remember him asking me to scratch his foot, the foot that had been removed (phantom pains). In his frustration "God damn it!" clearly resounded in the room. Andrew's home was room 109 for the duration of his stay. He had roommates come and go though little or no engaging in conversation with his counterparts. I wondered who was paying his bill. The hospital room cost at St. John's during that era was eleven dollars a day for a double room and thirteen dollars for a single room. Were hospitals expected to accommodate pro bono patients? Was pro bono a practice of religious affiliated hospitals only? Were patients like Andrew county cases?

    I had entertained thoughts of asking permission to take Andrew in a wheelchair outside on a warm sunny day. I never got around to it. What a pleasant surprise to spot Leslie, another aide, pushing bundled up Andrew, with a slight smirk on his lips, outside by the emergency entrance. Leslie had a family that kept her busy. I wished I had gotten to know her better. I wished I had gotten to know other co-workers better. With people my age off to their own lives, dances were no longer a draw for me. I depended on my parents for the use of a vehicle, so hospital life was my life. A few coworkers were bowlers in Long Prairie. Bowling didn't exactly excite me but I knew I needed entertainment away from my family and the hospital. My dad decided that bowling was not something he wanted his firstborn to do away from people he was comfortable with. So I returned to limbo.

Chapter Eight

By the second summer of St. John's existence numerous people had passed through the employee ranks as short-term employees. Many were after school and college students working evenings and through the summer. Several aides worked the night shifts and likely had their own stories, though we never met outside of work. RNs and LPNs filled in for maternity leaves, vacations or when Sister Jacquelyn was out for six weeks due to double pneumonia and staph infection. The summer of 1957, Yvonne, an RN, was hired as a full-timer, right out of nursing school.

The first year with the hospital was a most serious and focused year for me and I suspect the Benedictine Sisters, doctors and all hospital staff. The community of Browerville was proud of its newest addition, a rural hospital, and the staff worked hard as a team to get this endeavor up and running. People of all ages worked in cleaning, cooking, laundry, lab, x-ray and night nursing shifts. It was amazing that the daytime medical leadership on the floor was so young. Sister Jacquelyn, the nurse supervisor and anesthetist, was in her mid-twenties, RNs Janet and Yvonne were in their early twenties, and when I was brought into the surgery and nursery mix, our average age in those responsibilities was twenty-two-and-a-half years old. It was an era in society when most people were given jobs and then expected to figure it out, fit in or move on. I somehow managed to remain employed.

Shortly after Yvonne came on board a viral flu hit the community and its teenage and young adult victims were hit hard. I was no exception. Those weeks off work left me weak and sleeping much of the day. Recovery was slow. My mother was expecting baby number thirteen in September and the sisters again accepted my request for one month off to assist my family at that time.

On another occasion when hospital patient count was low and no major surgeries scheduled, a woman in our farm neighborhood with a large family was five months pregnant and threatening to lose her baby. Mrs. Gebhart was hospitalized and put on complete bed rest. I asked the sisters if the patient and her husband agreed, would it be okay if I took a few days off to assist the family. Permission granted.

I had my hands full and remember baking a birthday cake for one of the little Gebhart children for a weekday supper. The cake didn't rise as I had hoped, though I had an even bigger let down when informed that the Gebhart family celebrated birthdays only on Sundays. I had broken their family tradition.

It was well into the fall before Yvonne's and my relationship started meshing. Hers would be a different and much-needed role in my life. I had been totally immersed in Catholic living. Separation of Polish and German was the most I had been exposed to at that time. Occasionally a seminarian from our church would bring a person of color home for the holidays. Had I gone to high school I would have interacted with all caucasians and minorities would have been Lutherans.

The hospital had employed several people of other religions. Now there was Yvonne, a Lutheran and a supervisor. I was thrilled the day she pointed out on the cardex-file that a patient's religion was listed as "NP Cath." Yvonne wondered what that meant. I wasn't sure either, but I guessed, "non-practicing Catholic." Actually, I think I had reason to believe it was a good guess.

A significant number of hospital employees smoked. I had not. I doubt that any of the sisters did but who knows. Years later I met nuns that smoked. One day; alone in the nurse's lounge, the usual accumulation of lipstick-lined cigarette butts caught my attention. I decided to take the one that I thought matched Yvonne's lipstick color and practiced the art of smoking without lighting the Camel. The taste was horrible. The fact that I never went on to smoke cigarettes had nothing to do with having the discipline to stand up to peer pressure; I had no desire to engage in something so distasteful and I was getting serious about saving up my forty cents an hour income to figure out a way to move beyond Browerville.

Heaven only knew how that was going to happen. In the three years that I ended up working at the hospital I never once took my check to the bank. My dad banked in Clarissa, six miles from Browerville, and he deposited my check into a savings account in my name. I never withdrew money. I kept enough out of each check for charity, clothing, gifts, or to treat myself to something.

My first purchase to ruffle my mother's feathers was a light green electric circular Lady Schick shaver that I had seen in an ad on our new, snowy reception television. This was my first experience of buying something on time. Iten and Heid's Hardware accepted my offer to pay one-half down and they would hold the shaver for two weeks until my next payday. I never admitted to anyone that a straight-edged razor did a smoother job than my Lady Schick.

Shortly thereafter I went to Brenny's, a dry goods and grocery store, and purchased a very small three-piece set of blue luggage. Other girls were getting luggage for graduation and since I would have no graduation, I was going to have to make the purchase myself. My mother again was rattled and asked; "Are you planning to leave home?" My response: "No, just planning to do a little traveling." I had only "just in case" plans, nothing specific.

Something was changing within me. While I still lived at home, dependent on my parents for vehicles and food, I was finding ways of expressing my independence in small ways. Clarissa had a women's clothing and accessory shop that drew me in. Since working late was not unusual for me in the summer months, there was no need to believe I would worry anyone if I made a quick trip to Clarissa. I purchased an absolutely darling white with red Swiss dots shorty pajamas set for myself. I must have shown my mother, or else she checked my room, but Dad came to me and said; "We can't have those pajamas here in this house, with so many brothers and the sisters that I must set example for." (This was one of many episodes of an oldest child paving the way for younger siblings.) I told Dad that if my purchase was to go back he was going to have to be the one to return it. He did and he refunded my money.

    The day at the hospital was going as usual when I received word to prepare for surgery. Apparently Yvonne, who seemed fine in the morning, was going in for an appendectomy. When the surgeon had removed the appendix and was doing routine internal one- or two-finger exploring exclaimed; "What the heck is this? Is she menstruating?" Janet answered; "Yes, and she uses Tampax." (I was not privy to that information.) Tampax? I had seen boxes with that name on when I purchased feminine products. Now I started toying with the idea that maybe I would try them even though my mother had informed me that only one thing was to be inserted into the birth canal and that one thing was for the purpose of having children. I liked Yvonne and her values and was pretty sure that someday I would use Tampax. (I did! . . . after I moved away from home.)

    Yvonne invited socially-inept me to take a break with her at lunch time and rather than hospital food, we go to the local restaurant. I ordered a hot beef sandwich. What a treat! Another time Yvonne invited me to join her and a couple of other young women on a girl's day out and travel to Minneapolis and St. Paul. My idea of city life was of seeing June Cleaver in dresses and high heels at all times. I neglected to ask Yvonne how she planned to dress. I did my own thing, a dressy black sheath and black three-inch-heeled shoes. The others wore casual skirts and blouses with flat shoes. I managed to hold my head high and wobble around the downtown Twin Cities.

On our way home we stopped at a restaurant in Anoka. The place was crowded. A group of young guys sat at a table near ours and asked the waitress to give a note to me. The note implied something about my looking like a troubleshooter. I wondered what the guys meant by troubleshooter. I refocused my attention on the ladies and was exhausted when I got home. My reflection that evening was that of wondering if Yvonne actually enjoyed my company or was working with me in expanding my horizons. Either way I appreciated it so much.

Yvonne's boyfriend was from her hometown. I was invited to their wedding, a small Friday evening candlelight affair I was told. Catholic teaching of the day was that we Catholics were to get permission from our pastor before attending a non-Catholic wedding. I wanted so badly to attend Yvonne's wedding so I went and sought my pastor's permission. I did as told and my parents drove me to Eagle Bend and we waited outside the small white church until we thought the service was over.

With the gift I had carefully chosen in hand I went directly to the church basement for a reception with cake and coffee while Mom and Dad occupied themselves somehow. We agreed on a time for them to pick me up. Now I was convinced that I, with a huge family, wanted someday to have a small evening wedding. Catholics didn't have evening masses at the time so how this was going to happen, I couldn't imagine. First I needed to date someone, but whom?

Farming and small town dynamics, with nearly everybody knowing every move made by people of the community, did not appeal to me. Yvonne's influence was nagging at me. I was going to have to be patient. I went to the garage one evening where my dad was working and told him of my concern of how to go about leaving Browerville. He suggested that I wait until after mom had the baby in September and then think about going to the Twin Cities where some of his and Mom's siblings were living. Marie was born September 30. Winter came and spring followed and I continued living at home.

Chapter Nine

Staying awake during a night shift when all was quiet was no easy task. My night shifts were rare so adjusting my system's clock was a challenge. Drinking coffee with the RN, playing Solitaire, or wandering alone down the dark back stairs to the dimly lit basement for a snack from the kitchen at three a.m. were not my favorite pastimes. Entering darkened patient's rooms with a flashlight directed at our waists so as not to disturb patients, allowed for us to listen for patient breathing. Sometimes patients needed bathroom assistance or a sleeping pill. Surgical and obstetrical patients might require more attention. Usually, the middle of the night hours were painfully quiet.

    The upper cabinets to the back of the nurse's station housed blood pressure cuffs, stethoscopes, thermometers and miscellaneous supplies. Several shelves lay bare. One night I spied a single thick book on the top shelf of the middle section of the cabinet. I decided to investigate. I am tall and was able to reach it without using a step stool. It was a nurse's manual. Flipping quickly through the manual I discovered interesting human anatomy pictures with explanations. In the fifties human anatomy reproductive pictures were not included in elementary school training and only on a limited basis at the high school level. I heard the RN returning and replaced the book where I found it, planning to revisit this source of knowledge soon. I wonder what reaction I would have gotten if I had asked to take the book home or if my parents or siblings found the book at home.

On-the-job training provided an abundance of anatomy exposure. A call light went on for a gentleman who was on bed rest. He needed a bedpan. Intending to be attentive to keeping him as covered as possible while slipping the bedpan under his buttocks, a very large red scrotum got in the way. I stayed calm and returned to the nurse's station and reported what I saw to Janet. She thanked me for the information and shortly thereafter the doctor and Janet, with a small tray of necessities on a cart, headed down to the room from whence I came. Janet acted as though the procedure was something she was well-trained for. I tried a quick search in the nurse's manual. No luck. I got the impression that a needle on a twenty cc or larger syringe would be injected into the scrotum and fluid aspirated.

That was the end of the enlarged scrotal story until sometime later, my dad, during one of his many hospital stays, needed a procedure and the doctor, nurse and same type of tray and supplies headed for Dad's room and closed the door. Nothing was said to me, nor did I ask questions. Darn, I should have asked Dad before he died twenty-eight years ago. He would have told me the truth by then, I think, if he remembered.

One day I arrived for duty and it appeared we would have a quiet day. Only two small surgical procedures were scheduled and I would not be needed in the OR. The first case was a man that requested to be put to sleep to have a ganglion cyst removed from his wrist. He was returned to his room, and was displaying unusual restless behavior. He was given an injection of something to calm him down before the doctor and nurses returned to OR.

The second surgical patient was my dad who had frequently been hospitalized for spiked temps, cause unknown. The decision was made to remove his tonsils when in his mid-forties. Dad's tonsillectomy was taking much longer than those of younger patients. I attributed the delay to his age.

The ganglion cyst patient wasn't regaining conscious status as usual. It was as if he was possessed by a demon, thrashing around his bed fighting off something. No RNs were on the floor and all of we aides left our assigned patients to relieve one another in holding the patient down and trying to keep him from injuring himself or others. Finally I decided we needed help so I went to the OR and poked my head in the doorway planning to explain the situation to the surgeon and nurses. Dad's doctor loudly exclaimed; "What is she doing in here?"

It became apparent that things were not going as planned with my dad. That image of the operating table positioned in the middle of the operating room with blood splattered on the wall about ten feet away was another clue. I was informed to have the Sister Catherine from the lab come to OR for directions on what dose of medication injection to give to the thrashing patient. It must have been a strong dose of something. Shortly thereafter he was again asleep. It was quite awhile before Dad was returned from surgery . . . no explanations . . . no questions asked. The ganglion cyst patient slept a long time. RNs and the doctor were back on the floor when he did finally wake up.

While employees were sheltered from being too involved with immediate family members, some of us were from large extended families and with many friends. This meant there would be times that familial circumstances would require our involvement. One such time was when an aunt of mine was having a cholecystectomy. I was asked to scrub in to use both hands to grasp a crude retractor to hold back the liver so as to expose the gallbladder for the surgeon to see. This responsibility was a first for me.

With the internal part of the surgery complete, the retractor was removed and the surgeon commented that we were fortunate that the retractor didn't cut into the liver. There were signs that I may have been applying too much pressure. Once a patient was put to sleep and draped for the incision to be made, I was amazed at how, for me, a relative or friend was transformed into a patient that needed care, not someone I had emotional ties to. However, I am grateful that I was not in the operating room when my dad had surgery.

It was to have been a quiet weekend with few patients. The local doctor was out of town and both RNs had the weekend off. An out-of-town doctor was on call. Two obstetrical patients changed our plans. The first was a multi-para and delivered with ease. The lab technician was called up to oversee the floor in the absence of RNs. Delivery of the second baby, with complications, was taking a long time. The lab tech called me to the bedside of the first OB saying that she couldn't get a blood pressure reading.

I noticed that the stethoscope was positioned on a part of the arm that might explain the inability to hear pulsation. After repositioning the device, I pumped up the cuff. The reading was now sixty over . . . ? I checked for bleeding which I considered was an acceptable amount. When raising her gown to massage the fundus I discovered that the bump was nearly up to her ribs. I had never experienced a fundus so high. My heart skipped a few beats as I began to gently massage as trained to do. Large clots and blood and more large clots and more blood were expelled. One of us massaged while the other took her blood pressure.

The fundus lowered slightly and was firming up. The blood pressure was beginning to rise gradually. The patient, a friend of my family, was alert and conversing during our stabilizing her bleeding before the doctor and Sister Jacquelyn finished in the delivery room. A blood pressure reading of ninety-eight over

Millie Hoelscher Moran

whatever number allowed me to take a deep sigh of relief and whisper a prayer of thanks. It was surreal, as if the patient and we inexperienced staff people had been encased in a protective bubble. The angels were with us. Life went on as usual, or maybe not. Life became ever more precious to me.

Chapter Ten

The new St. John's Hospital attracted doctors and their patients from surrounding towns. Specialist surgeons came in from Brainerd for urology and genecology procedures that general practitioners were not trained to do. Some patients were sent to larger hospitals. Doctor Lenarz's dream had come true. He could focus on bringing improved patient care to our small town and I had the privilege of becoming a small part of the team that was set in motion.

In the beginning life at the hospital was very somber. As time went on we welcomed and instigated humor to balance the weight of heavy situations. One of those times was in the operating room. Doctor Fredrick Gross, a man with a big heart and short in stature, often assisted in surgeries. It was an ordinary event to bring a stool for him to stand on, after he was scrubbed and gowned. One day, after a long abdominal incision was made in the patient, he decided that he needed the higher of two stools. As he transferred from one stool to another he teetered a bit, crossed his gloved hands over his chest and exclaimed; "Freddie, you fall in and it will be gross contamination." I welcomed the controlled chuckle that was happening in my gut.

Gradually I was growing more comfortable with the doctors, nurses and myself in surgery. One day a patient that had lost a tremendous amount of weight, likely due to cancer, was asleep on the table with her legs up in stirrups. Sister Jacquelyn's routine responsibility was to intubate the patient for breathing purposes and was holding the patient's jaw and oxygen mask in place. I always admired how Sister sat at the head of the patient and positioned her eight fingers under the lower jaw to hold the head in place. With pillow removed Sister could let go with one hand to adjust anesthetic gasses or to chart information.

One of the RNs was scrubbed in and readying instruments in preparation for the doctors to arrive. My job was to use forceps, folded gauze and Merthiolate to prep the surgical area, in this case, for a vaginal hysterectomy. Neither nurse had commented on the deep lower abdominal creases due to weight loss. Painting with Merthiolate from the navel through creases on down to the table left me perplexed as to how I might proceed and do a thorough job. The normally serious me, asked if Sister Jacquelyn could tilt the patient's chin up and back a bit. The two nurse's eyes widened above their masks, quiet laughter ensued and their faces were beet red when the puzzled doctors sauntered into the room awaiting sterile towels to dry their hands before the gown and glove process. No questions or explanations were given. Somehow I felt like this was another right of passage. I survived initiation. I learned later that patients who appear to be asleep might hear conversation going on about them. Mea culpa!

Heavy somber moments linger in my memory such as a neighbor's farm accident, which resulted in a forearm being amputated. There was also Mrs. Langer, a hospital employee, who suffered a ruptured brain aneurysm and was brought to emergency surgery. It was going to take a miracle to save this patient that not even the doctors were trained to perform, especially in a small hospital setting. Surgery had begun. A round saw-toothed hand drill was used to make the opening through the skull.

The only telephone available in the operating and delivery room areas was a phone on the desk in the doctor's lounge. Dr. Lenarz, without breaking scrub, instructed me to accompany him in going to the doctor's lounge and I was to dial the number for a doctor at the University of Minnesota Hospital. I dialed. The doctor came to the phone and I held the phone to Dr. Lenarz's ear as he asked for guidance as to how he should proceed. The phone call ended. The two of us returned to surgery. Doctor requested fresh gloves. Little could be done. Mrs. Langer died later that evening.

Bernice was still awake on the operating table and as she was giving way to Sodium Pentothal. I told her I would be there to greet her when she woke up. Well into the procedure Sister Jacquelyn informed the surgical team that the patient's vitals were erratic. Her heart stopped during what was considered a minor

Millie Hoelscher Moran

lower abdominal surgery. A quick-thinking surgeon made an incision just below the ribs on the patient's left side, inserted his hand and massaged the heart which resulted in a rhythm returning. Bernice lived in a comatose state for a few days. I never again told a patient that I would see them when they woke up. It was another lesson in how fragile life is.

Chapter Eleven

Now a year-and-a-half, two years into employment I was still only earning forty cents an hour. Sometimes I wondered what other nurse's aides were being paid. I learned years later that federal minimum wage in 1956, the year I started at the hospital, was raised from seventy-five cents to one dollar an hour. There were exemptions for domestic work, farm work and very likely certain health care positions. I could have felt taken advantage of and maybe I did just a little because of all of the responsibility I was given and handling.

My dad had a cliché he used when we broke something or dented a car fender; "Education costs money." For me, this cliché applied to my work situation as well. With almost no living expenses due to residing at home, my savings account was nearing a thousand dollars. I fantasized of some day being blindfolded and with pencil in hand I would ask a family member to take the big globe and twirl it. I would place the pencil on the globe and wherever it stopped, except for Los Angeles (so near to Hollywood, the sin capital of the world) or behind the Iron Curtain, I would pack my bags and find my life out in the world. I was determined to hold that thought and to become financially stable before taking the plunge. I was convinced that God would protect me as I found some service to do in underprivileged areas of the world.

****

The sisters were becoming like family. A carload of nuns, clad from head to toe in white habits, made occasional visits to the farm. What a precious memory I have of watching Sr. Jacquelyn cradling a bunny in her hands. I silently hoped she would change her habit before returning to patient care.

On the flip side of this relationship, when I worked a summer Sunday three to eleven shift and was scheduled again for seven a.m. and surgery, I was allowed to stay in room 107 with a three-quarter bath so I could shower and clean up before going back out on floor the next morning. I couldn't do this during the school year.

Dad had an arrangement with the sisters and the high school coaches. While younger siblings rode the bus, the high school brothers could participate in sports and shortened practices if the school, hospital and family could agree on the boys helping with chores and Millie starting at the hospital at 8:00 a.m. (7:45 a.m. on surgery days) rather than 7:00 a.m. like other staff. In exchange, I would work later so the boys could practice basketball, baseball or track for awhile after school, not the entire practice because farm work was calling. The coaches were likely flexible because they needed players and the competitive brothers engaged in athletic activities on the farm whenever farming allowed. They were good and played well together.

****

With hospital and family working together for the benefit of both, I think I crossed over the line a couple of times. One time was after I had been hospitalized and my doctor prescribed Phenobarbital, ten milligrams before meals and at bedtime. On a few occasions, if I worked beyond what I was scheduled for and was going to be at the hospital for the supper meal, or if I forgot to bring the med with me, I went to the drug room, helped myself to the Phenobarbital and mentioned it to no one. After all, it was doctor's orders, I justified, and I believed all involved wished me to stay well.

In addition, heavy menstrual bleeding plagued me, and one of the sisters from the office informed me that I had bled through my uniform. I started wearing a half-slip under a full slip with a hemmed rubber panel made from a remnant of baby crib rubber sheet. With a heavy ribbon through the hem designed to tie around my waist, I wore the panel between the two slips. Still there were times I would use up the sanitary pads that I brought from home so would go to Central Supply and take a long OB pad without clearing it with someone, but whom? I considered myself doing what I had to be done and assumed I would be given permission to do so anyway. Maybe not!

At home I pulled pranks like getting up at 6:00 a.m. on April Fool's Day to sneak downstairs while everyone was still asleep and ring our long wooden old fashioned telephone that hung on the wall with our one long and one short ring, to be heard by all fifteen parties on out rural party line. Then I ran to the staircase and hid waiting for one of my parents to get out of bed and come to the dining room to answer what might be an emergency call. My heart was pounding so hard for fear of what my parents would say or do. Mom said "Hello" several times before I stepped out and hesitantly said "April Fool!" I wonder what people on the party line thought? I was never reprimanded for this antic. After all, there were worse things I could have done and my parents had performed "April Fool" pranks as well. They were my teachers. What could they say?

Among my parent's friends was a fellow that I considered someone that needed a prank pulled on him. Years earlier he had taken sexual liberties with me in broad daylight when I was playing hide and seek with peers. I went indoors and told Mom immediately. She hugged me and told Dad in the car on our way home, with me sitting between them. Days later Dad informed me that he had talked to the guy in the middle of Main Street in Browerville. The man denied it. Life seemed to go on as usual for people in my life. I believed this man deserved some form of retaliation. If I got caught I would fess up.

Like many people in the area this fella donated blood frequently. I still shudder to think that such a thought even ran through my head and then that I would act on it. I wonder if "The devil made me do it." I stopped off at the lab on my way to lunch. The lab techs were gone so I tore off a charge slip from the stack lying on the counter. Later that evening, at home, trying to disguise my penmanship, I filled out the charge slip with a fee for supplies used for donating blood. I used an envelope from home and stopped at the post office the next day and mailed the bill to the home of the man. Then I waited for ripples. Nothing of the incident ever got back to me. The incident became part of a future Saturday Confession.

****

Where would my life end up? The thought of becoming a nun or marrying someone from the area gave me a sense that I would be settling for someone to take care of me, either as a wife or a nun. While I loved my family I believed there was a need for some distance, at least for awhile, and that God loved me and I would make it out in the world somehow. I longed to take a calculated, or maybe not so calculated, risk and experience God's protection in a big way. I was naïve and not embracing the awareness of protection from a Higher Power on a minute-by-minute basis all of my life. I prayed to Saint Jude, patron of hopeless cases, to intercede to God for me regarding my future. Nothing was clear other than to continue with prayer and patience to discern more of what I might need to learn. Socializing was minimal. It was a prayerful desert time listening to the nudges within. There would be more learning at the hospital and participation in family life.

Millie Hoelscher Moran

****

When situations in the operating room were not demanding I remained nearby within earshot outside of the operating room. During these times I might clean instruments, wrap packs to be sterilized for surgery or delivery, make sure that enough gloves were sterilized in various sizes and rotate by length of time since sterilization date. One day I noticed that someone was placing a long stainless steel container into the autoclave and it dawned on me that I had been washing out surgery scrub brushes and I was tall enough to return the used brushes to the hanging container over the scrub sinks without brushes being sterilized. I told Sister Jacqueline about my oversight. Again, I was not reprimanded but if looks could kill; I'd have been mush. Lesson learned.

Family members took their turns being patients. Eight-year-old brother, Allen, had a tonsillectomy. The two siblings, Greg and Marie, that were born at St. John's when I took a pre-arranged, non-paid maternity leaves to help out at home, came down with something causing severe diarrhea. It was just after Christmas. The hospital was filled to capacity.

Often there was role reversal between Mom and me. I was exhausted from a long day at work, and about bedtime my mom asked if I thought the babies should be hospitalized. I responded that I thought their condition warranted medical attention, leaving the decision to Mom and Dad. They packed up the little ones and headed for the hospital. I was relieved.

Socially Challenged

The next time the night nurse saw me she scolded me by saying that I should have known that the doctor needed to be contacted before a patient could be admitted. I assumed she would call the doctor. She likely was overwhelmed with patient count and would have to go to the record's room to find the patient number for the little tykes. The little ones were put in separate cribs in isolation. I was tied up in surgery several days during their hospital stay. I don't recall that our parents visited them. They would wait for me to bring home a report on how the two were doing. Thank God for other staff.

At the end of my shift I would go to these little people in isolation, and read what others had recorded on my youngest sibling's intake and output sheets. I remember the baby had thirteen stools recorded and the toddler had nine in one day. I longed for Mom and Dad to be with their little ones. Finally Greg was discharged. Arrangements were made for me to take him home but first to stop by the clothing store and buy him new shoes. I was reimbursed. Marie was discharged a few days later.

One Sunday after work I stopped at a family gathering. A relative was bold enough to ask if it was true that one of the three men hospitalized due to injuries in a head-on auto collision the night before arrived dressed in women's clothing. I told him I hadn't heard that, which was true. I worked the opposite end of the hospital and only knew which rooms the patients were assigned to. If the women's clothing rumor was true, I assumed it was the single man and not the two family members from the other vehicle.

The next day Sister Jacquelyn approached me and motioned me toward the alcove near the elevator where the wheelchairs were stored. She informed me that word had gotten out that patient in room 108 arrived dressed in women's clothing. She asked if I had leaked it. This was one time I was relieved to not know details. I was shocked. While not saying a word to anyone about the rumor I had assumed the wrong patient. I could honestly answer Sister by saying I knew nothing of what she was referring to. Thank you, God! When I returned to work after my two days off all three patients were gone.

While aware of numerous patient conditions, I was not part of every patient's care. Exposure to the information regarding patients was of value for me to better understand life. I knew we had a patient that had attempted suicide. I have no idea what method he used. He was comatose when I left work and gone when I returned. Not much turned my stomach but the thought of suicide did. I found myself reflecting on the fact that Jesus knew about people choosing to hopelessly end their lives and even Jesus couldn't, or didn't, stop Judas.

We also had a woman suffering from depression, probably postpartum depression. Her husband was with her. I remember her doctor shaking his finger at me and admonishing me to stay out of her room. A "Do Not Disturb" sign was on her door. My thoughts wondered and I hoped the activity behind the closed door would not lead to another pregnancy. She had her hands full as it was. Mom had suffered from nervous breakdowns and depression when overwhelmed with life. I didn't wish that on any family.

Doctor Lenarz was hospitalized after a heart attack. The RNs took his vitals and answered his call light. His wife, a nurse, was his primary care person. Certain patients were given more personal or private care. I was in cruising mode and ready for my next phase in life, or so I thought. However, there were two things I had not experienced and I wondered if it would ever happen. I had assisted in cesarean section births but I never witnessed a natural birth. I've wondered if the sisters or doctors had a reason for that or if aides simply weren't needed for the job. My parents didn't allow for girls to see calves born. Perhaps hospital supervisors were protecting us from the reality associated with childbirth.

Likewise, I was taught to give injections and did so only with orders by the RN in charge, nothing routine. I was never taught to start an intravenous feeding though often assisted, added units of blood or IV fluids. There was more I could have learned though I was ready to move on. Then came June 10, 1958.

Chapter Twelve

It was bedtime June 9, 1958. Bedtime prayer included thoughts of my promise to St. Jude a year earlier. I had been diagnosed with a digestive disorder and possible bleeding which led to requiring blood transfusions. As earlier mentioned, like the mother of the baby that required blood exchanges, it was discovered that my blood Rh factor was negative. If I would have children with a man who tested Rh positive, there was a good chance our babies would require blood exchanges and progressively worsening symptoms with each pregnancy. Having had blood transfusions, related information served as a forewarning that I was already sensitized and that each pregnancy or miscarriage would increase the likelihood of producing newborns that would fight the antibodies building in my blood. Mom's blood type was Rh negative and Dad's positive, yet they had no such problems. But it could happen.

My prayer petition and bargaining was that if I could meet a good, caring Catholic man and we were able to have a healthy baby, with my husband in agreement, the first baby would be named in honor of St.

Jude: Jude for a boy or Judy for a girl. The next day I was planning to attend a wedding of a girlfriend and I got up and personal with God saying; "It is time. I have been patient and I anticipate that tomorrow at the wedding I will meet the man I will someday marry." Kneeling during the wedding mass I may have whispered a prayer for the bride and groom. Mostly I was prayerfully preoccupied with how meeting my future spouse might evolve. No connection or sparks flew during the day. However, that evening, at the wedding dance, a couple of strangers to the Horseshoe Lake Pavilion were showing interest in our group of young lady friends.

The one who was home on leave from the military and a boyfriend of a bridesmaid asked me to dance and the other, a tall, tanned and over six-foot tall fellow, and not a particularly good dancer, danced with my friend. Later we switched partners. The tall dark, tanned gentleman was home from Los Angeles for his sister's upcoming wedding. He was to be a groomsman. I knew his sister's fiancé and his family. This guy would be in Minnesota for another month.

His family lived in Little Falls, approximately forty miles from Browerville. He asked if he could take me home. My dad's admonishment vibrated loudly in my mind. "If a guy meets you at an event and asks to take you home, he likely has one thing in mind. If he is genuinely interested he will ask for a date." I declined the gentleman's invitation. He asked for my phone number. I gave it to him.

Some days later there was a phone call but the connection was such that Mom was unable to hear the message. She presumed it had something to do with my brothers returning from out-of-state seminaries for their summer vacation. I told her it was probably the person I had met at the dance. Mom was stunned.

Dad and Mom were at the wedding dance where Don and I met. Out of concern, they changed their plans for leaving the dance early and leaving me to go home with a relative. Rather, they drove me home. My supposedly non-prejudiced mother informed me that she thought the guy showing interest in me appeared Mexican. It sounded as if Mexican was contrary to her preferences. We had never met Mexicans or dark-skinned people. (Don was a California beach-tanned Frenchman.)

A few days later, to my surprise, this person named "Don" was at the door of the hospital at the end of my shift and asked if I would like to get something to eat. I agreed and told him that I had just received a phone call from my mom asking me to stop by the train depot and pick up two trunks that belonged to my seminarian brothers. I asked if he would first be open to stopping by the depot and bringing the trunks back to my vehicle. He agreed. Don was driving a beautiful, shiny dark green 1950 Oldsmobile convertible with the white top down. I wondered if the trunks would fit in the car or probably scratch the paint.

At the depot we were informed that Dad had just left with the trunks. Puzzled, we ventured out into the side street by the Browerville Clinic. To my dismay, at the stop sign, my dad was in his pickup directly ahead of us. I doubt that he checked his rearview mirror and recognized me in the vehicle following him. Heaven only knows how that scenario might have played out if Dad had spotted his firstborn in the snazzy car with a stranger.

After the stop sign Dad turned out onto Main Street and went north, while we went south to the local Dairy Queen. Don asked if he could pick me up later that evening at the farm and that we go to a movie in Staples, twenty miles north. I was on board and at peace with my decision. At home Dad was in the garage. I had been rehearsing how I would break the news of my plans to him. While Dad was considered strict, I much preferred going directly to him with information than going through Mom. He and I had a mutual respect for one and other's spiritual convictions and reality. In my opinion; Mom often overreacted to new information.

I anticipated a positive response so went to the garage where he was welding. Dad stopped what he was doing. I said; "Remember almost a year ago when you asked me to remain at home until mom had the baby and then go to the Twin Cities to find work and maybe I would meet someone I would like to date? Well, I don't have to leave home. I've met someone and we are going to the movie in Staples tonight." No questions or admonitions from the family patriarch.

Millie Hoelscher Moran

When Mom arrived home from shopping I was making supper. I don't remember how she learned of my plans for the evening. I do remember being concerned about being embarrassed over the chaos that went on in our large family at mealtime and cleaning up afterwards. I excused myself from the table and went to prepare for my evening. Don arrived, came into the house, met a few members of the family, seemed comfortable in his skin and we left for the movie.

At the theatre and with a bag of popcorn we settled in for the movie *Peyton Place*. Midway into the story there was a scene regarding incest. It is one thing to learn sexual information with hospital situations but I was quite uncomfortable absorbing this cinema story probably rated R (I hadn't checked), with a strange man. I asked if we could please leave assuming that this would be the end of our relationship. We left.

It still amazes that I went with him not knowing his last name. As we drove home we passed the sign for Moran Township, between Staples and Browerville. Moran happened to be Don's last name. Don asked if I would care to go to his sister's shower dance on Friday night. A parental dating guideline had been that dates are to be at least one week apart. Friday was only three days away so I declined. June is Daylight Savings Time so the sun hadn't set when we got home from Staples. I invited Don in to meet more of the family. We sat in the kitchen with the crowd overflowing around the table. I was impressed with how comfortable this nineteen-year-old Californian resident seemed with this crew of farm people and likely farm odors. As he left, I followed him outside and told him that if he were still interested, I had changed my mind and would go with him to the shower dance on Friday night.

****

There was no reason for me to be embarrassed by my family's chaos. When we got to his family, that household left me stunned. Don is one of ten children, six girls and four boys. My sisters were young and calm. That would not describe Moran girls. One of the girl's was married. The rest were borrowing clothes, yelling to one another and putting on a scene that was totally foreign to me. If my brothers fought, I was unaware of it. My family was German, mostly blonde and fair skinned. The Moran's were half French and very attractive. Don was a male amidst females and the situation in my family was vice versa. Our family landscapes were miles apart.

We enjoyed the night of dancing and returned to Browerville about midnight. I welcomed his goodnight kiss. We made plans for me to go with my cousin to his sister's wedding ,ten days later on a Monday. In the St. Cloud Diocese, our diocese, a Catholic wedding with a wedding dance had to be held on a weekday. No Saturday night dances were allowed so people would hopefully be sober and alert for Sunday mass.

The Moran wedding was enjoyable, with a dinner and evening meal in the church basement and the reception held a few blocks away at the bride's parent's home. I remember kegs of beer being consumed that day. Don got unusually loud for a while. Without telling him, I had decided that if he got drunk, I would end the relationship and go home with someone else. I would have relatives at the dance. He had the good sense to limit his alcohol intake. We left the dance early for his eighty-mile roundtrip drive.

Driving allowed for pleasant conversation that included our shared family faith traditions. My parents were born and raised Catholic. Don told of his dad being raised Catholic and that his mother was never baptized into any religion. Don is the fourth child. The first four children were baptized. Don continued that his dad worked long hard days and started going fishing Sunday mornings so they could have fish for meatless Fridays, as was the Church rule back then.

Don's story continued. His paternal grandmother prayed that before she died her son, Chauncey, and his family would all return to the Church. Don was age fourteen when a phone call came that his Grandma had a heart attack during the night and died knowing that the next day her wish was to be granted. Don's unbaptized mother and younger siblings would be baptized and others like Don would receive their First Communion, as did his mother.

It was obvious that conversion process had left quite an impact on Don. This Californian wore a Miraculous Medal on a chain around his neck, a gift from his mother when he departed for California at age seventeen. He supposedly had Catholic friends in California and attended Sunday mass regularly.

Socially Challenged

During his remaining two weeks in Minnesota, Don met some of my extended family. The last week before he left, while parents objected, we went on four dates. We would see each other a maximum of ten times that summer. During that final week Don made the comment, "When I come home next summer, we can get married." I almost choked with thoughts of; "Yeah, right! You are going to be in California and I will probably never hear from you again." He gave me his high school ring with a black onyx stone to be a reminder of him in his absence. I was unsure if I would commit to wearing the ring. He sold the convertible needing cash and returned to California with his uncle.

The letters started arriving once a week and then twice a week as he made plans for a return visit for Christmas. The dating was replaced with letter writing and once a week I would cut narrow white adhesive strips to layer inside the bottom of his ring and shellac it with clear nail polish. I preferred this approach to wrapping a half-inch thickness of adhesive tape around the shank. Tacky? Maybe.

I felt connected to Don. I missed him like I had never missed a non-relative before. Besides, the ring meant there was no need for explaining my non-dating status. However, a seminarian friend of the family, a few years older than me, stopped by with his brother to visit. He asked to see the ring. I gave it to him and he proceeded to force the tape out. I seldom get fired up in my chest. I was angry and told him "I think I hear your mother calling." His family's farm, as the crow flies, was about twenty miles away. My dad had a good laugh.

The seminarian gave his brother the car keys and encouraged his younger brother and me to go for a drive. I left just to get away from Herb. Actually, I would like to have dated this seminarian studying theology, philosophy and psychology, all subjects I was interested in learning more about. I squelched that thought before meeting Don. I didn't want to remotely consider the possibility of a soon-to-be-ordained priest leaving that path and becoming my husband. I could envision marriage squabbles and a husband expressing that he should have stayed on the journey to the priesthood.

This may have been the beginning of numerous community efforts, and possibly with my parent's knowledge, to lure me away from any thoughts of moving to points unknown. Herb was ordained, officiated at the wedding of my sibling and then left the priesthood, married and moved out of state to share his gifts in a capacity other than as a priest.

****

Since I hadn't gone to high school, I had no class picture taken. Without telling anyone, that fall I made an appointment with a professional photographer and ordered pictures to give my parents, grandparents and Don framed five-by-seven photos of me. The new Betty Crocker Cookbook that I ordered had arrived in a sturdy box. The framed picture for Don fit into the cookbook box perfectly for safe shipping. Don teased me that I was just trying to not so subtly let him know that I could cook. Not true. I could cook and, yes, I wanted Don to have a picture of me. I was beginning to think I would possibly be leaving the state the following summer and I wanted my family to have a professionally photographed picture of me as well.

Chapter Thirteen

Doctor Brown, his wife and their little girl arrived in Browerville shortly before Don and I met. Health care in Browerville was booming with enough clients to keep two doctors busy. With the distraction of my new special friend in California, life at the hospital and at home became more of a blur. My body and emotional state must have been in a positive place as well. The months following Don's departure, my once erratic menstrual cycles turned into predictable twenty-eight day cycles. Awesome! My health was the best it had been in years.

Federal minimum wage was raised to one dollar an hour in 1956. My wages continued at forty cents an hour well into 1958 and after Don left. When I had been wearing Don's ring for a couple of months, the sister from the office that wrote the checks informed me that my pay had been raised to eighty cents an hour. I responded with "Thank you" and there was no more discussion. Secretly I wondered if the visual signs of the possibility of my moving away might have had an impact on this decision.

Socially Challenged

In the 1950's, verbal positive strokes were not the norm in my culture. Being given more responsibility and handling it was received as a vote of confidence for me. I do remember one day, for whatever reason, the hospital was filled to over flowing in patient capacity. Surgeries, births, emergencies, admissions and discharges kept RNs from their usual perch at the nurse's station. Aides were so busy resulting in patient's baths that generally were finished by lunchtime dragging into mid afternoon.

If possible, patients were given partial baths or a basin of water and soap and towels to give themselves a bath. An additional RN was called in. The nurse's station desk was cluttered with charts that doctors had left when making rounds. All of these charts needed RN or LPN follow up. One of the RNs managed to take a break from surgery responsibilities to distribute noon meds. Record keeping of admissions and discharges were in total disarray.

Other than entering something minor to a chart, charting was not something that I would or should have done. The seven to three-thirty shift had ended. The nurses and aides that came on duty at three o'clock were pulled in multiple directions. Sister Jacquelyn's shift routinely went from 7:00 am until 7:00 pm. It was obvious that charting would not be ready for the evening report.

Concerned about what other aides would think about me sitting alone at the nurse's station assuming a self-imposed responsibility, I hesitantly decided to work beyond four o'clock and simply try to the best of my ability to sort through the mish-mash of paperwork, so that a qualified person could get a sense of what went on the floor during the day. Individual lists of admissions, discharges, patient complaints and activities along with what I considered pertinent information was left in an obvious place at nurse's station in hope that patient's charts could be updated adequately to prevent as much confusion as possible.

When I left for home, no nurses were in sight, only the three to eleven shift aides, and I have no idea if added help came after I left. The following day Sister Jacquelyn motioned me aside and thanked me for the job I had done to make her charting easier. She worked until ten o'clock that evening. That compliment was a huge relief and affirmation.

Another vote of confidence came when the RN, Yvonne, asked me to do her a favor. I seldom gave injections. An acquaintance of Yvonne's was a patient. I didn't know the whole story. The patient was adamant about needing a hypo for pain. Apparently not enough time had lapsed since the previous hypo so Yvonne prepared a placebo injection and sent me off to the designated room.

In as much of a professional manor that I could muster, I sauntered off to the patient as if I had done this job routinely. With the injection sight alcohol swabbed, I proceeded to give the injection. The patient commented; "You are good at giving shots." After dozing for a while, he reported feeling much better. This was not my proudest moment.

Socially Challenged

****

*M*rs. Ronkowski was returned from surgery on a gurney and positioned in the bed in her assigned room. Our small hospital had no recovery room. As usual, I was assigned to stay with her for post-op observation, checking her vitals and getting her to verbally respond. Suddenly her blood pressure plummeted. I pushed the call button and lowered the head of her bed. Knowing a response could take more time than the patient might need, I rushed out of the room, passing family members waiting out in the corridor to nurse's station.

Thankfully, Dr. Brown was writing orders. He rushed to the patient's side and ordered me to get a certain vial of medication from a cabinet near the operating room, likely something the anesthetist would use, plus a sterile syringe and needle. I drew a blank and informed him that I knew nothing of what he was talking about. While the situation was critical, it was actually a relief to admit to not knowing and fumbling my way through a situation and losing the patient. Dr. Brown briskly exclaimed; "Where is Janet?" I responded, "She is taking her break." After all, this was routine post-op care.

I went to the nurse's station, dialed the lab phone in the basement and requested that the lab tech locate Janet in the dining room and explain the urgency. Time passed in slow motion. By the time Janet reached the patient's room the blood pressure was edging upward. I don't remember exactly what happened after that other than the patient lived. I believe that the greatest impact of that incident for me was that there is a time to assume responsibility and a time to admit to not being qualified, especially in life and death situations.

****

*A*pparently Doctor and Rea Brown had reason to think that I was responsible enough to care for their two-year-old and three of Mrs. Brown's nieces for a weekend while the two sets of parents went to South Dakota. It was my weekend off at the hospital so I agreed to watch the children and thought it would be a little extra money in my pocket.

The three nieces ranged in age from two to five years old. In my family there were always siblings old enough to assist with childcare in the parent's absence. The four little girls and I had never interacted before. I was exhausted trying to figure out their personalities and they mine. Meals, naps, baths, outside activities and picking up toys were a three-person job and I was a lone adult, young adult. I draw a blank as to how I got to church that weekend. Perhaps family members relieved me so I could fulfill my Sunday obligation. I can't imagine not attending Sunday mass.

The final day when the parents were due to return home I thought I could trust the girls to stay in the backyard while I made the beds. It seemed just a few minutes but when I got outside the girls and their dog were missing. I walked around the outer perimeter of the house, to the garage, the basement and immediate neighbor's yards calling the oldest girl's name. Nothing!

Panic stricken and wishing that a sibling or two of mine were at my side with extra pairs of eyes, ears and legs to act as detectives in locating these preschoolers, I whispered a prayer to St. Anthony, patron of finding lost articles, and raised my gaze beyond the immediate neighborhood. Good grief! The four girls and their dog had crawled under a barbed wire fence to a nearby pasture where a herd of cows and a bull were grazing. I was ready for the parents to return . . . STAT!

When the parents did return, the pay was much less than I expected from a doctor. Perhaps the doctor wasn't as wealthy as I had assumed. My decision was made. Carrying for children outside of the family for a living would definitely not be my avocation. The next day I returned to work at the hospital exhausted, but relieved. The children were delivered safely to their parents, thanks to their guardian angels and mine.

A few days later in surgery Dr. Brown was talking about his sister-in-law with three little girls and pregnant with number four. He mentioned that her doctors were beginning to think that she ovulated twice a menstrual cycle. In those days Catholics relied on the Rhythm Method for spacing children. This method assumed that ovulation occurred on or around day fourteen of the menstrual cycle, leaving no room for hormonal imbalances. My inquisitiveness soared.

I desired to learn more about ovulation and fertility. Living on a farm offered some clues. Parents with thirteen children meant that more research was necessary for me. Years later I trained to become a fertility awareness instructor and learned that a woman might have more than one egg released during ovulation, though not days apart. I was beginning to get a sense of how various experiences, observations and journeying with others was laying a foundation for choices that would impact my life.

Chapter Fourteen

A noticeable shift was taking place within me that last quarter of 1958. While still connected to the Community of Browerville, the hospital and my family, the ebb and flow between attachment and detachment was settling in. There was a growing sense of confidence and desire to prepare myself, and the family, for my eventual launch from the nest. When the seminarian brothers left a few years earlier it was like a death had occurred in the family. I was now several years older than the boys were when they left and I hoped my departure would be easier on my parents and the family.

Dad was talking about applying for a loan to purchase a piece of machinery. For some reason (my idea) I decided to offer him the eleven hundred dollars that I had saved interest-free, with a verbal agreement that when I needed the money he would get it to me on short notice. I had been living at home, paying no room and board, using parents' vehicles and gas from the five hundred gallon farm gas barrel located near the machine shed. We never discussed my contributing to family expenditures. No outside force dictated that it was payback time. I simply believed this was the right action to take. Dad accepted the offer.

****

A small package arrived in the mail addressed to Mildred Hoelscher. What a pleasant surprise. It was from Don, a gold cross and chain. I learned that Don went to California planning to attend Los Angeles City College. When the older brother he was living with was drafted into the Army, Don, with a year and a half of Community College behind him, quit school to support himself. He found employment at an upholstery shop. His job was to remove automobile seats from vehicles and prepare the seats for a facelift. If articles found in cars were from used car dealerships, the employee was free to keep the treasure, in this case, the cross. So he purchased a fourteen karat gold chain to compliment the cross. I cherished it as a reminder to keep my focus on the goal of preparing for a geographical shift to another culture.

****

Out in the community people I least expected to take notice of my activities were making comments about my changing life. While giving a patient a bath she mentioned she hadn't seen me, and my boyfriend, at Horseshoe Lake dances in awhile. Inquiring as to what she meant by boyfriend, it became obvious that she was referring to my seminarian brother, one year younger than me. Prior to Len leaving for the seminary at age seventeen and again when he was home for Christmas and summer breaks, he would drive us to dances. We loved dancing together, especially to the instrumental "In the Mood." The patient sold tickets at dances and commented, "He paid for your admission." She seemed amused by the explanation that I gave Len fifty cents on the way to the dance to cover my admission cost. He was handsome and I was delighted to be considered his girlfriend though that was not the goal. I simply didn't want to carry a purse and I enjoyed dancing with him several times an evening.

Len and I practiced dancing in the living room and like other brother and sister couples at local dance halls, we were pretty good dancers. One Saturday morning, house cleaning day, I had just scrubbed the living room floor, a nine-by-twelve foot piece of bordered linoleum with an area rug-type design that was laid over a painted hardwood floor. I set the bucket with water just outside of the living room door and Len came dancing into the living room, awkwardly tripping and falling onto the bucket. I could have been upset but it was a hilarious sight. Poor Len was embarrassed. These are pleasant memories. At age twenty I rarely attended dances. In addition to Don living two thousand miles away, my peers had moved on to college and work. Such is life.

As relatives and others learned of the male friend in California, I on a few occasions heard comments implying that since I was so sheltered as a young person I would likely go wild once I got on my own. Inspired by an article in a Catholic teen magazine that I read in adolescence, I made it a bedtime practice to pray three Hail Mary's daily for guidance to live life in a wholesome manner. I learned that when I sincerely prayed for something regarding making choices, I was more inclined to remain focused on my goals. Those comments about me becoming wild made me more determined to set high standards for myself.

One day I stopped at the post office to purchase a book of seven-cent airmail stamps. Regular stamps were three cents and it took about a week for delivery. Airmail letters reached Don in three days. Spud was at the post office window. He had been our rural mail carrier for years. When giving me the stamps he questioned; "Is something serious going on in California?" Both Spud and the postmaster played in a band that frequented area dance halls. People were watching! I was taught that as the oldest child I was always to remember that younger siblings were watching my example. But people were watching, period! Having a long distance relationship appealed to me; I shuddered at the thought of small town scrutiny. In retrospect I believe that my environment served as a support and accountability cradle that made my life simpler.

****

It was Advent. For the first time the hospital sisters offered a selection of Christmas wrap, ribbon and cards for sale. This was perfect! Never before had I purchased a gift for every member of my family. Because this might be my last Christmas at home I was devoted to making a special effort in planning farewell gifts that holiday season. Usually I gave only Mom and Dad and a sibling godchild gifts. This year most of the gifts were token items, like earmuffs for older brothers to PEZ candies for younger siblings. Len was the only brother remaining in the seminary. He had so few clothes and I chose to give him a brown and white-stripped shirt, which seemed to go over well. Black bow ties were the trend that year among younger guys. I bought one for Dad. Judging by his reaction he likely never wore it even though he wore suits, white shirts and long ties often. For Mom I purchased a size eighteen dress thinking it might motivate her to loose a couple of pounds. She had very thin legs but with all of those pregnancies her tummy was like a firm barrel.

Don was expected at my home on December twenty-first. I knew the day he was to leave California. He checked the Los Angeles Times want ads and located someone wanting a passenger to help drive and pay half of the gas. The fella was en route to Winnipeg for the holidays. I waited all day the twenty-first and twenty-second. The plan was for the two guys to drive straight through. Those were a couple of very long days with no word from Don. Finally his dad called. Don had checked in with his family indicating that the travelers had gotten caught in a Wyoming snowstorm. It took twelve hours to travel from Laramie to Cheyenne, a distance of about fifty miles. Don's concern was his agreement to pay half of the gas costs for their mode of transportation, a 1953 Cadillac convertible. With storm and mechanical conditions the car was guzzling gas faster than their wallets might be able to handle, and

Millie Hoelscher Moran

Don had two weeks before returning to warmer climate and a paycheck.

When he finally reached the farm our embrace in the laundry room of the house was more than I could have imagined. I didn't care who saw us. It was such a relief to see him safe and to look forward to our two weeks together. I left with the two young men for Little Falls. With winter driving conditions, arrangements were made for me to spend a couple of nights with either Don's relatives or my girlfriends who shared an apartment. During the holiday season we Christmas shopped and spent time with both of our families. Family expectations for Christmas Eve, Midnight Mass and Christmas Day gatherings were an eye opener. There was no way to please both families. We tried to be fair.

One pleasant moonlit night Don's parents loaned Don their car to take me home. It was about midnight. We were a half-mile away from my home when the car ran out of gas. I suggested that I would feel safe staying in the car while he walked to the farm to ask my brothers to get him some gas from the farm gas barrel. Don exclaimed, "I can sit here as long as you can!" So we walked home together, me in my skimpy slip-on shoes and his gloved hand holding mine. Don could have spent the night at the farm but his dad needed the car the next day for work.

On the twenty-ninth, the day Don was to leave, he again picked me up with his parent's car. We returned to Little Falls together. In broad daylight we parked on a side street to have a few minutes alone together before he left with his sister and brother-in-law for Minneapolis to catch his train back to Los Angeles. As my honey was about to head out the door of his parent's house he turned back and we kissed like two lovers about to be separated by war. The door closed. The house was quiet. Don's dad exclaimed; "I thought for a moment there were going to be two people leaving." Then he and Don's mom drove me back home and met my parents. Next I was to begin making plans to go to Los Angeles at Easter time to determine if L.A. would be a place I would consider living.

Chapter Fifteen

As 1958 turned into 1959, sponge counting and surgery responsibilities continued as before. During extremely long surgeries one of my responsibilities was to make arrangements with the kitchen to prepare nourishing malts for those of us confined to the operating room. That was an interesting exercise. Sister Jacquelyn could manage to drink her malt without assistance. One at a time those scrubbed in would step away from the table and I would have to lift the top tie of their mask and turn it around to the back before offering them the malt with a straw for them to sip from. Next the masks were to be returned to the original position and surgery continued.

On slow days I would get to interact with routine post-op and OB patients. I relished my reputation of giving great back rubs and tightening the ten-inch wide OB binder securely around the new mother's abdomens to hold the fundus and large OB pads in place. One day after Rosie's binder was pinned securely in place I was leaving her room and immediately the call light went on over her door. She informed me that although there was no pain it seemed the binder was pinned to her shrinking belly skin. Sure enough, a pin had gone through a layer of stretch mark. Mea culpa! . . . Again!

Mr. Johnson, although perhaps not deaf, had hearing issues. As was routine when taking afternoon vitals of temperature, pulse and respirations, we were to ask the patient if they had had a bowel movement that day and indicate the response on the clipboard's list of patients. Mr. Johnson was in room 110 near the diet kitchen and nurse's station. When I asked him the bowel movement question he peered at me blankly and grunted "huh." I repeated the question a little bit louder and annunciated hoping he would read my lips. Again he grunted and again I spoke louder. Finally I closed the door to his room hoping staff, patients and visitors would not hear our verbal exchange. With that he nodded his head with a response of "Oooohhhhh, yes, one!" and the smirk on his face told me he was playing a game.

Joan, a young wife that I admired from town, delivered her first baby. With wedding and/or engagement rings on my scope of dreaming, I was attracted to her unique wide wedding band with no engagement ring. I loved the simplicity of the one ring and it seemed practical. If Don and I were to marry, we were going to need practical. Traveling back and forth across country was depleting his savings. My values continued to be formed and influenced by my encounters with people, mostly at the hospital. I hadn't gone to high school or college, though life experiences had a major impact on me. People were mentoring me and probably didn't even know it.

Millie Hoelscher Moran

****

One afternoon when I was twenty years old I had gone upstairs to my room to sort through the clothes in my closet and chest of drawers. With arms full of clothes to pass on to others I returned downstairs to the kitchen and found Mom slipping something behind the bib of her apron. She had a sheepish look on her face. I addressed her saying, "You are reading Don's letter, aren't you?" When I opened my mail I placed it upright on the second glass shelf to the side of the window above the kitchen sink, planning to take it to my room later in the day. This day I had forgotten to do so. At first Mom denied it, though later admitted to reading the letter. The next Saturday after going to Confession she informed me that she had talked to Father Kraemer in the confessional about reading my mail and that Father told her that she and Dad had done their job of raising me and now they were to trust in God and me to make decisions for my life.

In late January, Mom had a doctor's appointment with Doctor Gross regarding a lump in her breast and the concern that it might be cancer. She tried fitting into the size eighteen dress that I had given her for Christmas. Mom only wore dresses, never pants, even at home. The dress from me didn't fit so she found something else. Upon her return from the doctor she asked me what I thought the doctor had to say to her. Out of the blue, as if with a sixth sense, I retorted; "You are pregnant?" She stuttered and stammered and said; "No, I mean about the lump. He said it was likely a plugged milk duct."

Socially Challenged

Later that evening Mom pulled me aside and informed me that "yes," she was pregnant and would I please go upstairs to the trunk and get that black dress. That black dress. The non-descript blah dress that appeared early in her previous three pregnancies, that was my inside clue or her way of taking me into her confidence before other siblings were told that she was expecting. That black dress was Mom's interim dress, worn between regular clothes and maternity clothes for a few weeks during her first trimester. Mom always exploded quickly and her already rounded tummy quadrupled in size during pregnancy.

One evening, early in February, Mom and Dad went to the hospital to visit Mom's sister, a patient. Upon their return Mom went to the bathroom. She called to me to come in and listen. I listened and stated; "What is it? You are urinating?" She responded, "No, this isn't urine." In checking the toilet, although mostly clear there was some bright red blood. Dad and I returned her to the hospital immediately. She was admitted and put on absolute bedrest.

Losing some sleep that night with the next day being my day off of work I assumed household and childcare responsibilities. Mom's activity was going to have to be very limited. The membranes had ruptured (her water broke). With three pre-school children in the house and several more riding the bus or driving to school it was obvious that once again Mom was going to have a baby and I was volunteering to take a maternity leave. I informed Dad that I was willing to take off work from the hospital beginning immediately with the condition that within two days he would have a new clothes dryer installed. Farm machinery it seemed to me always took priority over household appliances and furniture. With my recent loan to Dad to purchase machinery I felt justified to be firm about the dryer. I could be firm and gentle when speaking up to Dad in ways that Mom never thought of doing. Dad went into town that day and installed the dryer the following day.

The first day of using the dryer I washed fourteen loads of clothes. Prior to a dryer we females hung some clothes outside on the clothesline in the winter where they froze stiff as boards. We also ran clotheslines throughout the house main floor and basement. Family members dodged between flannel diapers and a plethora of articles. Hanging wet laundry indoors served as humidifiers in dry Minnesota winters. On this day in February and with Mom still in the hospital, the laundry, expect for the basket of clothes that needed ironing, was folded and put away. Now I could breathe again for a few days and ponder how Mom's condition might affect my plans to fly to California the end of March.

Chapter Sixteen

*B*efore Mom could be discharged from the hospital, Dr. Brown ordered a special corset for her from Santa Monica, California. I could have been inquisitive about what the expensive undergarment was supposed to achieve. My thoughts, however, preferred to focus on finding a map so I could determine how close Santa Monica was to the two cities I had mailed letters to the past months, West Los Angeles and Culver City. I knew Don had frequented Santa Monica beaches. Sure enough, all three adjoined one another. Thus began my becoming better acquainted with the geographical surroundings that might one day become familiar to me.

Mom was gaining back her strength and gradually resumed simple household tasks. Occasionally a call came from the hospital requesting that I come for a few hours to assist in surgery. If life at home allowed for it, I would make the trip to town. It was a welcomed break from large family life. Without my requesting it, I was given my second pay raise in three years, both within the last three months. This time the amount went from eighty cents to a dollar and five cents an hour. I wondered what was going through the minds of the administrative staff. Even at this higher rate my sporadic work hours resulted in checks so minimal that no income tax was withheld. The check stubs never reflected regular hours or overtime hours worked, simply TOTAL EARNINGS, OLD AGE BENEFITS, U.S. TAX WITHHELD, TOTAL DEDUCTIONS and NET PAY. I never questioned the hours not being listed until years later when I came across the check stubs. I considered my three years of working at the hospital as receiving compensation for learning about life in a safe environment. "Education costs money."

It was as if Don and I were functioning in a state of limbo, waiting for some indication that I could feel free to leave the family for a couple of weeks. This could happen only when siblings would be on Easter vacation and could help hold up the home front. I longed to visit Don as we had determined when he left me after Christmas. One Saturday morning in mid-March I overheard Mom having a phone conversation with her mother. I got the impression that Grandpa and Grandma and their two youngest children were leaving for the Twin Cities within a few of hours to visit their married children. I swallowed hard a few times, said a prayer and got Mom's attention. "Please ask Grandma if they would have room for me to ride with them to the city and if perhaps a relative could get me to the airport the following morning." Mom appeared dumbfounded, though asked the question on my behalf before informing Grandma that we would get back to her.

Socially Challenged

I was told I would have to go to the barn to get Dad's approval and some guidance. It was Saturday so our bank was closed. Somehow we had learned that airfare on Northwest Airlines from the Twin Cities to Los Angeles would be two hundred and fifty dollars round trip on a DC 7 propeller-driven plane with a stop in Salt Lake City. Dad decided he was comfortable giving me two signed blank checks from his account. The following Monday he would transfer funds from my savings account to his checking account to cover the cost. I packed my small three-piece, never-used luggage set with what this inexperienced traveler considered essentials. Within two-and-a-half hours I was dropped off at my grandparent's house just a mile from my home.

The nearly-three hour trip on Highway 10 to my aunt and uncle's house in Brooklyn Park is a fog. I don't recall feeling nervous. I felt safe with the arrangements being made. Don was unaware of my plans until I called him Saturday evening from my relative's home. He would be available to meet me at 2:35 pm at the Los Angeles airport the next day. Throughout the evening hours in Brooklyn Park it was decided that Uncle Francis would drive me to the airport after the seven o'clock mass the next morning. Mom's youngest sister, Clara, two years younger than me, would join us. I would be the first in my immediate and extended families to travel on a commercial plane. Aunt Marge, in her concern, suggested that someone drive me to the nearby Woolworths to buy a fake engagement ring to replace

Don's class ring on my left hand. She thought I might be safer if people got the impression that I was unavailable. I passed on that idea.

****

The alarm went off. Clara and I rushed to get ready for church and packed my luggage into Uncle Francis' little gray Ford coupé. We chose to refrain from eating breakfast so we could go receive Holy Communion and then buy breakfast after purchasing my ticket at the airport. I was amazed that the ticket agent allowed me to write a two hundred and fifty dollar check signed by a third party. The airport was much smaller than I envisioned. We located a restaurant and I internally agonized as to whether I would offer to pay for our breakfast or assume that Uncle Francis would want to be a gentleman and pick up the check for three breakfasts of ham and eggs. I had very little cash on my person and decided to save my money for possible necessities for the coming half month. In retrospect I wonder if Uncle Francis, Aunt Margie and their three children had to forego essentials due to my assumptions.

Once in my seat on the plane, flashes of self-doubt left jitters in my stomach. My biggest concern was Dad's signed blank check in my purse. I decided to trust in God and Don to get me through the next fifteen days. With the check shredded into micro-mini pieces, I, as inconspicuously as possible, deposited the lint-like residue into the ashtray in the arm of my window seat. I was flying first class champagne flight which meant being seated with all other passengers, though my meal would include champagne. Alcohol was not my thing. I had never consumed a full glass of wine, a bottle of beer and definitely not hard liquor in my entire life.

When the stewardess offered me champagne I decided to act experienced and sipped on the first glass. During a banquet-type meal with china, cloth napkin and fancy silverware, I was offered a second glass of champagne. I nodded, yes, and that too slid down smoothly. When my glass was being filled a third time, I declined and left the unfinished champagne to rest on my tray. I was wearing shoes with three-inch spiked heels and the plane would be landing in Salt Lake soon.

Marilyn, from Mankato, sat next to me. The two of us, both dressed in black sheaths, engaged in small talk and checked out the Salt Lake airport together. Back on the plane I jotted a few lines on a postcard addressed to my parents that I had purchased during the stopover. As the plane wobbled over the mountains between Salt Lake and Los Angeles my thoughts were tripping over each other. Marilyn was planning a two hour layover at the airport until her grandparents would arrive from Phoenix and show her some of the LA sights. She was open to killing some time at Don's apartment that he shared with two other guys. I was too numb to appreciate my first glimpse of the Pacific Ocean. Mountains were to the one side and ocean the other. My shallow breaths were caused by my anticipation of how Don and I would locate each other at the airport.

Millie Hoelscher Moran

LAX was larger than MSP thought not as large as I expected. I looked out the window. People were waiting on the tarmac for their loved ones. I exhaled a sigh of relief as I wrote the last sentence on the post card. "And there is Don!" I would mail the postcard the first chance I would get, with no plans to contact my parents throughout the duration of my vacation. Marilyn joined us in going to the apartment. Don's buddies returned her to the airport in time to meet her grandparents.

After freshening up, Don took me in his bright yellow '55 Chevy to show me where he worked, and we got a hamburger and a float at an A & W Root Beer Drive-In before arriving at 1424 Connecticut Street near downtown Los Angeles. This was Don's Aunt Claire and Uncle Mike's home, which would be my home for the next fifteen days. Don introduced me to his relatives. His cousin, Sherry, would be my bed partner. My visions of Los Angeles living were based on 1950s floor wax commercials or television's June Cleaver and Harriet Nelson in black and white. I needed an immediate attitude adjustment. I was exhausted and slept in late the next morning. Don had to work on Monday and picked me up after work.

Chapter Seventeen

My vacation home was located a few feet away from houses on three sides. In its day, during wartime, it had been a boarding house with four bedrooms, with a long hallway from the front door to the back of the facility where the two shared partial bathrooms were located. One had the toilet and the other a sink and a claw foot bathtub. There was a living room, dining room, a kitchen, four bedrooms, and front and back porches all on one floor. In addition to Sherry living with her parents, so did her older brother and his three pre-school-aged children, who were being raised by the grandparents. Thank God I was from a large family. I seemed to fit right in.

    The first week I stayed close to the house interacting with the children. I was out of my comfort zone, though gradually got up the courage to walk to Alvarado Street that took me to the church. Attending mass gave me a sense of being home. When Don picked me up after work it was already dark. By the time we got to his house one of his roommates had cooked dinner. Don was the delegated dishes person. Don washed

Millie Hoelscher Moran

and I dried. One evening the roommate asked if I could make gravy. I only had experience cooking for fifteen to twenty people. There was a bowl full of leftover gravy that got flushed down the toilet. By the time Don showered it was time to take me back to Los Angeles where we could chat awhile before walking me to the door. One evening he informed me that he had a phone call from his brother, Leo, requesting that Don be his best man for Leo's Saturday, July twenty-fifth wedding in Minnesota. We hadn't made definite wedding plans. Don would get only a one week paid vacation from his job. A trip to Minnesota and back would mean two weeks off, plus he was required to do two weeks of Army Reserve summer camp in August without company pay. Could he and we justify going that long without income?

Southern California had experienced a rainy winter. The green yards, majestic palm trees and flowers I had never seen before were beautiful. Don worked until noon on Saturday. The weekend was spent seeing sites that included Grauman's Chinese Theatre in Hollywood, the Conservatory at Griffith Park, the ocean and everywhere we went, people watching. I was introduced to Corvettes, just to observe, no rides. Saturday evening we went to Mulholland Drive at the edge of Hollywood. It overlooks Manderville Canyon on the west ridge and Canyon Back Ridge. Overlooking the lights below was amazing. In movies, dating couples would go to Mulholland Drive to park. Ours was one of several cars on the ridge that night. It was a wholesome enjoyable evening, the two of us alone.

My conditioning since childhood left me aware of the intrinsic desire for good. The question stirred in me "What is the good?" I loved being curled up in Don's arms and it was apparent that he enjoyed it, too. My three daily Hail Mary's beckoning Mary to intercede for me and now Don, too, to make choices that we would not regret took on a deeper meaning. I understood that even though we were not married or sexually active, we were already parenting. Choices I and we would make now would impact our future children, whether or not we married.

That evening when we were parked out in front of Claire and Mike's house our cuddling got rather passionate. We learned that it is one thing to pray for the strength to wait with sexual activity until marriage and live two thousand miles apart, and another to be together every day for a couple of weeks. We also learned that God was with us in a weak moment when Don proceeded to unzip the zipper on the back of my dress. It was a heated moment and the zipper got caught about a third of the way down my back. For a while I was beginning to wonder if I was going to have to wake Aunt Claire or Sherry to assist me. Eventually Don managed to get the dress zipped up. By that time we had calmed down. Lesson learned. We called it a night. "Thank you, God."

The next day was Palm Sunday. Don picked me up and we drove back to Culver City where we attended mass at Don's church, Saint Augustine's. I was introduced to his friends, the Faucher Family, who had taken him in as one of their own. We joined that family for Sunday dinner. The Fauchers were from Winnipeg. It was becoming apparent that Sothern California people in the 1950s were primarily transplants and thereby family. I was feeling drawn in and at home. That evening Don inquired as to what I thought of getting married on July 27, a Monday, and two days after his brother's wedding. That would be three weeks before my mother's problem pregnancy due date. Eloping was a temptation though our Catholic and family traditions would be jeopardized and our desire was to remain in the good graces of both. There was no guarantee that Mom's pregnancy would not throw our plans to the wind. We would simply move forward and see what would happen.

During Holy Week I passed hours sitting in a rocker on the front porch reflecting on whether my marrying Don would be a form of running away from something or going toward something. It is difficult to explain the sense of peace I experienced. Throughout my teen years I relished Scriptural stories of Moses, Noah, Abraham, Joseph, Ruth, Sarah, Mary, Joseph and Jesus and all of their lessons of patiently moving ahead in faith and trust. My own grandmother who left Germany in her twenties, never to see her parents again, had a major impact on me. Anne Frank, Helen Keller and movies about heroes of all kinds left me comfortable moving on to a new life and trusting the outcome.

****

Socially Challenged

I have no memories of flying back to Minnesota. As planned, I had not contacted my parents throughout the vacation. With less than fifteen dollars in my purse I had to figure out how to get back to Browerville. At the MSP airport I arranged for my first ever taxi ride, with my destination being the Minneapolis Bus Depot. At age sixteen, after helping Aunt Marge and Uncle Francis following the birth of Larry, I was put on a bus to return me to Browerville. This final leg of my first trip as an adult was coming to an end. After the taxi and bus fares there was no money left for food. When dropped off at Dan's Café, Browerville's bus stop, I asked to use the phone to call home. Dad would be able to pick me up in fifteen minutes. I was happy to learn that mom was doing well.

Dad dropped me off at the house while he parked the car in the garage. I rolled Don's class ring around so it looked like a plain gold band on my ring finger. When Mom asked, "What news?", I did a mean thing and raised my left hand for her to see. She painfully exclaimed; "Millie, you didn't?"

Co-workers at the hospital must have gotten word that I was home. Within a day or two after my return, Yvonne called from work asking if I had any news. On the telephone party line I disclosed that Don and I had made plans for a July 27 wedding. That meant only three-and-a-half months to prepare for the event. I did not receive an engagement ring and was making plans to try and borrow a wedding dress, anything to save money.

Millie Hoelscher Moran

During my next stop at the hospital, Sister Fidelis from the office informed me that I would be receiving two weeks of vacation pay for a total of eighty dollars, my first paid vacation and I didn't even ask for it. With that I could justify purchasing a wedding dress that was actually mine. Shortly thereafter I travelled to Little Falls to visit Don's family. Don's mother commented that my skirt waistline seemed a bit large on me. I suspected she was concerned of the possibility of a pregnancy.

The first Saturday after my return I went to Confession, "Bless me Father, I am not sure if I have sinned. I may have caused my boyfriend to . . . on and on . . ." Father Kraemer, who likely recognized voices behind the confessional screen, stopped me and admonished me to not be so hard on myself and he gave me absolution. I was grateful and got back to writing letters to Don with news like: "I patched twenty-two pairs of blue jeans today." My farmer dad and brothers were very hard on jeans and unlike today's 2012 fashions, every hole or tear had to be mended. Next it would be necessary to collect my thoughts as to how to move forward with planning a wedding and moving to California.

Chapter Eighteen

Sunday evening masses were happening in California. To my knowledge, such was not the case in Minnesota. With all of the complexities of Mom's due date, Leo and Joyce getting married two days before us and Don having to report for Army Reserve Summer Camp at Camp Roberts, California, just six days after our wedding day, the logistics of planning a wedding was not exciting. A simple evening mass in the middle of the week with a cake and ice cream reception would have been fine with us. There would be one problem . . . how to keep a reception small with our large families?

As was customary, my parents would pay for the wedding and they had their idea of how the wedding would go. The mass would be at 10:00 a.m. The wedding party would rush to Long Prairie for a quick photography session and be back to the church basement for a fried chicken dinner at noon. Mom's dancing and card-playing women friends would prepare meals for two hundred guests. The friend's daughters and a few teenaged relatives would serve as waitresses. The reception would be out at the farm and then back to the church basement for a ham supper. We preferred to have no dance, though Dad verbalized his thoughts of how many free wedding dances I had been to in my life, and he thought that I owed it to the people of the community to have a dance. We didn't know how we would pay for a band. Don's dad decided to cover that cost while my parents made all of the food and beverage arrangements.

It definitely became a wedding of what the parents wanted. Don's sisters were my attendants and wore long, full-skirted dresses. Mom disapproved of the sleeveless bodice so Don's older sister retrieved some fabric from the under layers of the skirt to sew little capped sleeves. We survived and were grateful to leave our families on good terms, or at least we think we did. Heaven only knows how out-of-town guests filled their time in and around Browerville between the ceremony, meals, reception and the dance at The Clarissa Ballroom.

One heart breaker was when Dad informed me that I could not invite my hospital cohorts because the extended family was so large. So we, the bride and groom, made plans for a stop at the hospital to visit with staff and my cousin, Jim, a patient who was on complete bedrest, the result of a fractured spine, who would be unable to spend the day with us. The hospital friends gave me a kitchen shower and the sisters gave us wedding gifts of hospital down pillows with St. John's Hospital hand printed at the edge of each pillow, plus a Last Supper picture. I painfully accepted these special memory items that I wished could have been brought to the celebration by the guests themselves.

One former hospital employee friend living in the Twin Cities at the time sent a large painted figure of the Virgin Mary. It arrived in pebble-sized pieces. I sent her a thank you note though made no mention of the condition of the statue. No neighbors were invited. Mr. and Mrs. Parish from the farm adjacent to my family's farm came to the marriage ceremony and afterward outside of the church came to the newlyweds and slipped a five dollar bill into Don's hand. My heart ached. I was grateful.

Mom pulled me aside the morning of the wedding and encouraged me to take care of myself in my marriage. She went on to stress her belief that she was the one responsible for taking responsibility for the care of the children, house and garden led to her having major health problems. What did "take care of myself" mean? I remembered a couple of times that Mom let Dad know that she had had enough of his actions. Once was a Sunday morning after mass. My parents had been bickering about money issues. Mom had told Dad that the boys' Vaseline Hair Oil for greasing down their hair for church was in need of replacement. They had words. The silent-treatment followed. After church Dad made a u-turn and parked in front of Janusek's Drug Store and told Mom to go in and buy the hair oil. Mom refused. Dad made the purchase.

Another time I remember Mom washing out messy diapers in a bucket of water in the side-yard.

Dad was, in his mind, being playful and driving too fast toward her. He delighted in scaring family members with tractor and horses antics. Mom yelled for Dad to "STOP," and in frustration she picked up the bucket of floating BM and threw it at the tractor. It was not a pretty sight. Dad got her message, stopped and made no comment. Later she told me that she could not believe that she resorted to her actions. Little did I know on my wedding day how Mom's advice and permission to take care of myself would play into my self-care in the years that lay ahead.

Dad was awfully quiet the morning of the wedding. He was shaving at the bathroom sink when I asked him if he had qualms about Don being good for me. He answered; "Isn't it better to go slow and grow to like someone rather than be all gushy about a person in the beginning and then after awhile can't tolerate them?" His words guided me in future relationships.

Cherished memories of the day include getting dressed at my grandparent's home in Browerville. Aunt Margie, Mom, Grandma and Clara assisted with buttoning my gown, pinning the veil to my hair, taking pictures and holding my dress and hoop up off the ground when walking through two neighborhood yards rather than travelling the one city block by car. The bridesmaid's dresses were pink so I had purchased pink cotton fabric and asked Grandma to sew dresses for my sisters Jeanette, eleven, Kate, ten and Marie, two. The girls were so cute, thanks to Grandma.

I got word later that Don's family had their own preparation concerns. The tuxedos for both Moran weekend weddings were the trending black trousers and white jackets. Both Don and Leo had their tuxes hanging in a doorway at their parent's house. Unsure of exactly what happened, on the morning of the wedding Don rushed through the chaos amidst his family only to discover that his white shirt was missing, with assumptions that Leo had taken it. Don's mother frantically hunted for and ironed another shirt she found in the house. The black handkerchief for the jacket pocket was also missing. The Morans hoped there would be a clothing store in Browerville. There was Brenny's dry goods store, though no black handkerchiefs. They, being innovative, purchased a small piece of black fabric and folded it in such manner that the bride had no idea of the less than perfect attire that the groom wore.

Clara and my cousin Ann Marie opened and displayed gifts for a short time at the reception. Gifts were boxed up and stacked in the back seat of the car before we left for the dance. Don, the upholsterer, had sewn a vinyl tonneau cover to conceal the gifts. Knowing our travel circumstances, most guests gave money, which we used the following week to purchase two aluminum kettles, a frying pan and a coffee pot. Luggage was placed in the trunk and we were free to slip out of formal clothing and rest for a half-hour before readying for the dance, a dance we would have preferred to skip and be on our way, California bound.

Millie Hoelscher Moran

The dance started at nine o'clock. Only beer and soft drinks were available at the bar. Dad was already pouring whiskey into the glasses of mix and passing out cigars. He seemed to be enjoying himself. The grand march for the wedding party was scheduled for 9:30 p.m. We marched in and danced the traditional bride and groom dance, said farewell to a few people and left to return to the farm and change clothes. Dad kept pouring drinks and Mom drove home behind us. She needed to physically send her first born off to a land foreign to her, a land where her daughter would in a few days be alone while the new husband left for two weeks of summer camp. Don started the car. Someone had gotten into our supposed locked car and threw oatmeal throughout the interior and put limburger cheese on the manifold. Don quickly recognized the odor, stopped the car and cleaned the manifold as best possible.

Our first night was spent at a motel . . . an old motel in Sauk Centre. We took turns showering. Showering was good. Our parent's houses had bath tubs and no showers. I, in my new light blue knee-length gown, settled on the bed and waited for Don who returned from the bathroom showered, shaven, dressed in briefs and a t-shirt with an air of Old Spice. Crawling under the blankets I could hear my mother's voice, "Just take slow deep breaths." Good advice. Thank you, Mom. I do remember thinking "Is this as good as it gets?" and "Until death do us part."

The next morning I awoke to some spotting. When telling Don I was concerned about the bleeding because I had menstruated two weeks earlier, he gently informed me that he understood it was normal for a woman to bleed following the first time of intercourse. I hadn't read that far in the marriage preparation book that Father Kraemer had given to us to read and discuss since we were apart and unable to attend the six Sundays of Lent at marriage preparation classes sponsored by our diocese. Don informed me that in "guy" lingo it told the guy he had gotten a cherry.

In the marriage manual it was referred to as the breaking of the hymen or the maiden head, the tissue that partly or totally covered the external vaginal orifice. It explained that this tissue could also have been broken due to athletic activity or the use of tampons. Don went to the Rexall Drug Store to purchase sanitary supplies for me while I freshened up and packed my belongings. We drove for an hour before stopping for a breakfast of ham and eggs at a small town restaurant.

Chapter Nineteen

This first day after the wedding could hardly be called a honeymoon. We enjoyed being alone together, sitting joined at the hip to travel as many miles as possible each day to get me settled in Los Angeles before Don left for Camp Roberts five days later. 1959 was before seat belts and air conditioning in vehicles. In addition we struck out on our journey with no water or food to sustain us should we have car problems in areas with long stretches between towns.

Don did most of the driving. I drove for an hour so he could rest his head and close his eyes for a few minutes before taking the wheel again. Prior to meeting Don I had never driven in a community with a stoplight. A couple of times after our meeting I had driven alone to Little Falls to visit his family. The population of Little Falls was eight thousand people and it had only one stoplight. In 1959, there were no interstate freeways between Minnesota and California, only two-lane highways. This was going to be quite an experience for me.

The temperature reached 104 degrees in South Dakota that first day. At a gas station we purchased a bottle of Coca-Cola for Don and a Nesbitt Orange Crush for me. When we finally stopped in a small town with one gas station, a greasy spoon restaurant and a motel we decided to spend the night. Don spotted a hand water pump away from buildings. He used the metal cup chain-attached to the pump and guzzled down at least two cups of water, maybe more. At the café he ordered a beer before his meal arrived. All of a sudden he dashed outside. When he returned he informed me that everything he had consumed on his empty stomach came back up. Then we went on to eat a full meal with no regrets.

    After winding down in the motel we showered and readied for bed. I didn't have the courage on our wedding night to ask. This second night I asked Don if he would feel comfortable to continue a tradition that my parents and paternal grandparents had practiced throughout their marriages, the tradition of saying a Hail Mary together at bedtime asking Mary to intercede to Jesus for us to have a happy and blessed marriage. Don agreed and our bedtime ritual was set in motion. This was very comforting for me. I was journeying into many unknowns beginning with the trip. Then I would be alone in Los Angeles for two weeks while Don served Uncle Sam, of course anticipating a lifetime of marriage to a relative stranger, and a life in major contrast to my first twenty years of existence was cause for justifiable concern. The next day would again bring several hundred miles of driving.

    Ten o'clock Wednesday morning we were driving in the Black Hills and our car was surrounded by deer and a bear that came up to the car. We kept the windows up and moved slowly so as not to hurt wildlife that wasn't so wild and to stay safe, ourselves. The road through the area was dirt, as was the small parking lot. Few people were to be seen and we managed a quick glimpse of Mount Rushmore's four presidents. Urged on by a date with the Army Reserves, we had to continue on and maneuvered our way down to US 30 and eventually US 40 in anticipation of our destination of Provo, Utah. That meant driving all day and all night before stopping at a motel to sleep during the hottest part of the following day in the desert.

    Don may have had a map in the car, though he didn't use it. He had been across the country often enough that he knew the route he wanted to take. I don't recall much of Wednesday after leaving the Black Hills until about midnight, when Don announced that he was too tired to drive and asked if I could take the wheel for a couple of hours. Drawing from learned home and hospital challenges I decided I could handle it. There were no radio options in this remote area to help keep me alert. It was pitch black with no roadside lights and few signs on the road to guide us. Occasionally short sections of low metal roadside railings were spotted on the curves. Don cautioned me that I would be driving through mountainous area and to be careful of possible falling rock. With my response of "okay" he curled up in the passenger seat and slept.

    When he awoke, the first words out of his mouth were, "How is it going?" I reported that I heard a rushing sound as I was curving around narrow bends of the road and had glanced in the rear view mirror to see if rock was falling onto the road behind us. I saw nothing other than black. At the same time I spotted a "Beware of Falling Rock" sign. I whispered a prayer and wished that I had seen the terrain in daylight. This was my first time in the mountains. I managed to stay calm. Don took over the driving responsibility at our next stop. We continued driving and found a motel about dawn, earlier than we intended to stop. We needed sleep.

Unable to sleep any longer, we got up and packed by ten a.m. During breakfast we decided to drive through the beautiful area of Provo, Utah, and then make our decision about whether to attempt to cross the desert during the day. Actually, I left the decision up to Don. I had no understanding of Death Valley temperatures and risks. Still no beverages or food with us, about two p.m. we ventured forward. The engine was acting very dependable. With windows open we enjoyed the blue skies. I saw nothing pretty about the brown landscape with cactus and mole hills. Simultaneously, we became aware of the fact that something was odd. This was the middle of the day in Death Valley, the hottest month of the year. It was eerie. There was a white cumulus cloud overhead shading us from the heat of the sun for about an hour and a half. When the cloud lifted we were uncomfortable for a short time before reaching Barstow and Route 66.

Following a break in Barstow and getting some much-needed nourishment, we continued on. Passing near San Bernardino, Don informed me that if traffic cooperated we would reach Culver City and his apartment in two-and-a-half to three hours. Don pointed out a sign to the city of Riverside and that he had an uncle living there. A ways further I saw a sign for West Covina and knew my mother's cousin Jean lived there. We were far away from family yet with a sense of being connected to a lifeline if the unknown turned into a nightmare. Then of course, Aunt Claire and Uncle Mike lived in Los Angeles and when the other newlyweds, Leo and Joyce, found their way west, they would be living in Don's apartment. The furniture Don had belonged to Leo and rather than storing it while serving two years in the Army, Leo asked Don to keep it for him until he returned. I would stay in the apartment until Don returned from camp.

    The next two days were filled with emptying the car of clothes and wedding gifts, opening checking and savings accounts in both of our names, my new name, Mrs. Mildred Moran, and then getting on with life. The apartment complex had a coin operated laundry facility that I wanted to learn how to use. Prior to marriage Don had his laundry done professionally. I needed groceries and wanted to find my way to church, which was about ten blocks away. Don informed me that since he could not justify the cost of renting a garage, he parked in the street. If I didn't move the car every three days in his absence, it would likely be towed away. That was enough of an incentive to get out of the apartment and become acquainted with my new environment.

Saturday had arrived. Roland was to pick Don up at three o'clock, in time to get him to his Reserve Headquarters in Gardena before trucks left for Camp Roberts. We did some unpacking of wedding gifts, cleaned up the apartment and decided to take a nap before Roland arrived. We must have left the door unlocked and fell sound asleep. The next thing we knew Roland was standing in the bedroom door telling us he rang the doorbell. Don had to hurry. Our goodbye was more like, "I'll see you soon."

Chapter Twenty

Sunday morning, Don's friends picked me up to attend mass at St. Augustine's Church. Throughout the following week I tried to balance my day with various activities. With washing machines running it made sense to begin writing thank you notes to wedding guests. Between other loads I sauntered across Venice Boulevard to the neighborhood grocery store and picked up a few essentials, lingering in the produce department to observe fruits that were a precious commodity growing up on the farm.

I was thirteen when I asked Mom if I could please have a whole banana. She was surprised that I never had the privilege of such luxury and told me to go to the pantry to eat it so no siblings would request the same. Bananas were saved for Sunday and sliced into strawberry Jello. If company joined the family for dinner, the Jello would also be topped with barn fresh cream that was whipped. I purchased two bananas. Mom would eat half of an orange for every breakfast. The other half was cut into half sections and always the question; "Whose turn is it to have a piece of an orange today?" One orange went into my shopping basket. A half-dozen produce items I didn't even recognize.

Each of our families got a letter from me that week, my new weekly resolution. I took inventory of cabinet contents hoping to get a sense of how many boxes would be needed for moving. It was useless. I had no idea what belonged to Don or Leo. Each day I took a walk through the neighborhood. Another resolution I had made for living married life in a city was to attend weekday mass once each week in addition to Sunday. Feeling extremely brave I took a map with me and drove to Los Angeles in search of Aunt Claire and Uncle Mike's house. I made it just fine. Aunt Claire told me later she thought maybe I was pregnant because I was frequenting the bathroom. I am guessing it might have been a minor case of honeymoon bladder. Thank goodness it cleared up. I had no idea where to begin looking for a doctor. I found my way back to the apartment.

****

Don hadn't called at all from Camp Roberts. The second week of spending the nights alone in the apartment, the phone rang numerous times. I could hear breathing but no one answered. That freaked me out. I called the Fauchers and eighteen-year-old Armande agreed to spend a few nights with me. So we were two stressed females. The calls ceased.

On Thursday, I was sitting at the kitchen table with the back door open. Leo and Joyce went walking by. I was so happy to see familiar faces and that they had arrived safely from Minnesota. I spent the next two nights sleeping on the sofa so they could have the bedroom. The two days gave us an opportunity to get somewhat acquainted. I remember Joyce cleaning out the coffee pot and wondering where city people disposed of coffee grounds. She was stunned when I suggested flushing the grounds down the toilet. Her conditioning had been that coffee grounds should not go into rural sewer systems. We both burst into laughter. Bye-bye coffee grounds. That was a pleasant ice breaker.

Don returned Saturday afternoon. A fellow reservist delivered him to the apartment. It was August 15, a holy day of obligation. Don showered and we went to evening mass before finding a motel room where we could become reacquainted. Don was exhausted.

As mentioned earlier, the first nine months of our relationship my erratic menstrual cycles became more predictable, arriving on a twenty-eight-day cycle. The three months between visiting Don in California and planning our wedding day, my cycles went crazy again. I menstruated exactly two weeks before the wedding and anticipated that by Rhythm Method guidelines I would be in the fertile phase for our wedding. Other than spotting the day after the wedding there was no sign of anything. I had no idea where I was at my cycle and longed to be able to understand my bodily fertility functions. That night in the motel my entire being responded to Don in a way I had never experienced before. I believed it had to be ovulation. I knew enough from the farm that at fertile time females respond very different than at other times of a cycle.

The next day we rented an apartment in West Los Angeles and moved in as soon as possible. Mail from home usually had a three-cent stamp on the envelope. About August 22, a letter arrived that bore an airmail stamp. I was leery of opening it. Airmail postage from home meant important news, maybe bad news. My baby brother had arrived on August 18, Dad's birthday. Mom and baby were both doing well. What a relief. I asked Don if we could justify the cost of a long distance phone call for the baptism. Don was asked to be the sponsor by proxy for Lloyd Donald. We called home.

I was beginning to feel nauseous in the mornings. One of my first goals was to research and find a family practice doctor. I went in search of a Catholic doctor who would hopefully share our Catholic values regarding contraception. There was a community hospital in Culver City that I preferred to ignore. In the yellow pages of the phone book I discovered that St. John's Hospital was in nearby Santa Monica. I called the hospital for referrals of family practice Catholic doctors on staff at St. John's that delivered and cared for babies. I was given three names. Dr. Sumption's name sounded a bit like Assumption, the day I conceived. I called his office and learned that, yes, he was Catholic, the father of six children and his oldest daughter was in the convent planning to be a sister. I made an appointment for a month later.

In that month Joyce informed me that she thought she was pregnant, too, and scheduled an appointment for the same time so she could ride with me. When I needed the car I would have to take Don to work and pick him up again in the evening. One day I drove to the Motor Vehicle Department to apply for a California driver's license. I was now officially a California resident.

Our pregnancies progressed. Joyce found a job in customer service at Grant's department store before Christmas. She sewed some attractive fuller tops for herself. Mom sent me one of her maternity outfits. I purchased another and made good use of Don's shirts.

I spent most days at the apartment. One morning a week I would walk to mass. We got word that a parcel was being held at the post office for us. It was our wedding pictures. On the way home from church I, desperate to see the pictures, stopped at the post office and with my rounding belly carried the heavy box six blocks home. Several times I set it down, take a few deep breaths and continue on. These would be Christmas gifts to family.

Another day I decided to job hunt. The telephone company wasn't hiring. I filled out an application at the Culver City Hospital for a nurse's aide position. This was more detailed than my Browerville Hospital interview. I remember a questioner and multiple choice questions. The only question I remember that likely left me unemployed was; "When admitting a patient and she told you she'd like her fourteen-karat gold ring with a one-karat diamond to be placed in a hospital safe, would I specify that the ring was as she said or would I document that it was a ring with a gold band and a clear stone?" I answered the former and decided later that was awfully gullible of me. St. John's didn't have a safe for patient valuables that I knew of. I never heard back from the Culver City Hospital.

    We had been informed that Don's forty-eight-year-old mother was seeing a doctor for what was suspected to be a large abdominal tumor. Two weeks later we learned that, like her two new daughters-in-law, she too was pregnant and all of us were due at about the same time. This would be her tenth living child. It was strange getting into the mindset of Christmas with little money and no chance of a white Christmas. I could relate to Mary headed for Bethlehem.

Chapter Twenty-one

A glitter-sprinkled door ornament consisting of three pine cones with gold ribbon graced the exterior of our front door. Inside the furnished apartment a very small one-piece nativity set rested on an end table next to a stack of Christmas cards we had received. No other decorations adorned our home for our first Christmas. With no car available to me when Don worked, our friend Roland shopped for me and purchased a pair of bowling shoes for left-handed people in Don's size. We managed to keep it a surprise from Don. Don responded to my hint and gave me a used Singer sewing machine so that I could begin preparing for the baby that Doctor Sumption said, based on my last menstrual period, was due April 20. I disagreed. I was sure when I ovulated and when I conceived. After all, with Don gone for two full weeks there was little room for guessing. I planned to buy thirty-six-inch white flannel yardage, cut it into one-yard squares and hem diapers as I had done so many times before for siblings.

With Minnesota time two hours ahead of California we dialed the operator to place calls to our parent's phone numbers. The circuits were busy. After early morning Christmas mass we tried again and still no luck. This would be the second time of hearing my parent's voices since July 27, our wedding day. The circuits continued to be busy so after several attempts we joined Joyce and Leo in traveling to the relatives' for dinner. Aunt Claire was an awesome cook and Uncle Mike sat in his chair, with his gallon bottle of hard liquor that he had received as a gift resting on the floor next to his recliner. Many times a day he sipped from the bottle. His speech slowed down throughout the afternoon, yet he managed to win in poker with an occasional proclamation of; "Well, I'll be go to hell in a hand basket." That day I learned to play Scrabble with the women in the group. We returned home in early evening and were relieved to successfully reach both sets of parents by phone. This was a Christmas gift to both our parents and ourselves.

New Year's Eve we drove to Hollywood to attend a movie. I wore the new maternity top my mother sent. The theater was far more elaborate than any I had ever seen. I left the movie to find a restroom. Not spotting restroom signs I went through the exit door. The door was heavy and slammed behind me. Panic overcame me. I was out in a chilly vacant parking lot in the heart of Hollywood. Pulling and rattling the locked door got the attention of a security person who allowed me to return. His words informed me that I could have broken the door. I was so embarrassed and if I didn't tell Don then, he'll find out when he reads this.

Millie Hoelscher Moran

Money was tight that winter. Don's one hundred dollars a week wages didn't leave anything for savings. I was very frugal when buying groceries and began to stash leftover change and an occasional dollar bill in the small red jewelry box Don had given me for my birthday. Rather than drying clothes in the coin operated dryer I hung clothes on lines provided for tenants above the garage. I was the only occupant to do so. The air was so smoggy I wondered how clean our clothes actually were. In typical Minnesota style I believed my mother would be proud of how white my laundry was so I snapped a picture and finished off the twelve exposure film, developed it and sent the snapshot to Mom. Generations before me believed that "You could tell a lot about a woman by how white her whites were." That is why back in Browerville we were taught to hang white sheets and pillow cases toward the road so passersby could make a positive judgement call of performance.

In the winter months it was dark outside when Don returned from work. One afternoon he returned early, although the sun had nearly set. When I asked the reason for his coming home at this hour, I assumed he wasn't feeling well, and he told me he had been fired. My heart leapt to my throat. Then he recanted and explained that Max, his boss, had called a meeting and informed employees that with business slow, he would have to shorten their work days and totally eliminate Saturday mornings, all without pay. This was not the sort of news an anxious mother-to-be wanted to hear. Don was home for one Saturday and returned to his regular schedule.

Don had gotten into the habit of bowling with the guys Saturdays after work and wouldn't call me. His carefree bachelor lifestyle still had a grip on him. Tuesday evenings were regular bowling league nights. If possible I would schedule doctor's appointments for Tuesdays so at Don's suggestion, when I picked him up after work I would be the score keeper for his team.

Ash Wednesday was upon us. I attended mass in the morning. That evening there was a knock at the door while Don was at mass. To my amazement two former nurse's aides from St. John's in Browerville asked to come in. They were from Clarissa and younger than me. I knew they worked part time at St. John's after school. I had no idea how they found me nor did I know they were Catholic. The two apparently decided to be adventurous and try living in California. They needed an answer to their Catholic question. They had seen shoppers in stores with ashes on their foreheads and they wondered if Ash Wednesday was a holy day and had they missed mass on a holy day? I never heard from them again and wonder where their futures took them.

My due date was drawing closer and we were living in adult-only apartments. It was time to start looking for a cheaper, unfurnished apartment and to shop for furniture. I contacted Dad and informed him that with all that was coming at us, we needed the eleven hundred dollars I had loaned him nearly two years earlier. He sent a check immediately. Our address once again became Culver City.

Millie Hoelscher Moran

We purchased new furniture that included a going-out-of-style five-piece blonde bedroom set, a living room hide-a-bed sofa, a chair, tables, two lamps and a round kitchen table with four chairs. Aunt Claire's grandchildren were old enough to sleep in single beds so we inherited a bassinet and a cream-colored six-year crib. Joyce had moved back to Minnesota and Leo moved in with us in the one-bedroom upstairs apartment for a couple of months and slept on our new sofa. His plan was to be in Brainerd with Joyce when their baby arrived and return again to his California job until he had one year of employment in.

The April 20 due date came and went as I expected. A year earlier I had told my mother that I could possibly be a mother by Mother's Day, 1960. The Fauchers had a surprise baby shower for me. Leo had flown back to be with Joyce. The only thing happening with me was that I was getting huge and waddled. Saturday, May 7, I made breakfast for Don before he went to work and I crawled back into bed. At 10:00 a.m. my feet and bright red blood hit the floor.

Normally I didn't call Don at work, as it was a toll call, but today I decided to do so and give him a heads up. We didn't discuss bowling but he didn't come home when I expected him at about 12:30 p.m. Finally around 2:30 p.m. he came in. I was still spotting and starting to cramp with lower back pain. Don had been bowling plus he informed me that some guy he knew originally from Little Falls, now married and living in Thousand Oaks, had stopped at the shop to see him. Don had invited the couple over to play cards that evening. What was he thinking? Jerry and Maryanne stayed until midnight. Concentrating on 500 was not easy for me. It was a struggle to be gracious.

We went to bed and slept a few hours. Contractions were getting harder and closer. My understanding was that labor for a first baby could be a long time and I would rather be at home than unnecessarily in a hospital. Don was lying still, though likely not sleeping. When I called his name he jumped out of bed.

At six a.m. we started for the hospital, a half-hour drive, in our only vehicle, a 1946 Ford with weak springs. We hit a dip in the street and I thought we might be delivering en route. I was admitted and prepped. Don left the hospital to attend eight o'clock mass at St. Monica's Church nearby. When he returned the doctor met him in the waiting room to tell him he had a son. The cord had been wrapped around the neck twice, though the baby appeared to be fine.

To keep costs down I agreed to have a bed in a ward with six other new mothers. Big mistake! We were next to the noisy swinging doors to labor and delivery. This was not a quiet, restful confinement. It was Mother's Day, May 8, and my calculations were right on the date. The doctor thought eighteen days late. Don called his parents from a pay phone in the hospital and learned that Joyce and Leo's baby boy arrived on May 4. Sunday evening Don took me by wheelchair to the pay phone so I could call my family. This was the third time of hearing my parent's voices since the previous summer. Hospital regulations allowed for only husbands and mothers to visit maternity patients. I think I emotionally shut down just to survive the chaos and loneliness.

By the time baby and I were discharged on Wednesday I felt fluish. The following Saturday Don decided to work in the morning. He would not be paid for the days he had taken off work and we needed income. The apartment reeked from a discharge odor. Don arranged for Roland to take me in for a doctor's visit. I had been cut too deep for the episiotomy, the sutures had burst and I had a serious infection. Where was my mother when I needed her?

It still amazes me that somehow I, the country bumpkin, learned of diaper service. Mom had admonished me to take care of myself, so I did. I located a diaper service company to pick up soiled diapers and bring fresh diapers to our apartment on Mondays and Thursdays. Simply getting myself assistance for six weeks gave my morale a boost. Although I was a bit hesitant about how sanitary the diapers of other babies might be, I had to trust. All went well.

Frequent doctor's visits and treatments got me back on my feet in time for baptism. The Fauchers were the proxy godparents for Don's parents. The baby's middle name was Jude, as promised to that saint a few years earlier. Don's healthy baby brother arrived May 14. The forty-eight-year-old mother was a roommate of a forty-nine-year-old mother. Such was small-town family life in the 1940s to 1960s.

Chapter Twenty-two

*I*nsulated by farm family life and limited education, I felt socially and emotionally challenged when moving forward into each new situation. Always, in addition to my own determination, someone or a situation would draw me into moving beyond where I had ever ventured. Now it was Chris, my next door neighbor. Her child, Stacey, and my RJ were just a few weeks old and it was time to get them started with immunization shots.

My parents had not taken immunization for children seriously. I believed it was a parent's responsibility though was unsure as to how we were going to afford this benefit. Chris, an only child, whose parents owned a home in Culver City, was planning to take her baby to monthly Well Baby Clinics sponsored for free by Los Angeles County. If it was acceptable to Chris and Art it would be suitable for us.

A stroller, a baby gift from Roland, provided many opportunities for pushing RJ alone or with girlfriends and their babies throughout Culver City. The Baby Clinic and City Park were a few blocks away on

Overland Boulevard. A trip to the bank or shopping center required walking on the sidewalk along the outside perimeter of the MGM Studio lot. When I was alone I felt a bit vulnerable though adventurous. We always reached our destinations safely. "Thank you God."

Although our apartment complex had a single coin-operated washer and dryer, sometimes I would prefer to pack up my baby, laundry in pillow cases plus detergent, and trek via stroller six blocks and past the park to the Laundromat. Once when leaving the facility I spotted a man's wallet just off the sidewalk. What to do now? After checking for the address within I decided to take it home with me and attempt to contact the name on the identification card. There were a few smaller bills in the wallet.

That evening Don was home to stay with RJ. I couldn't locate the name in the phone book that corresponded with the name on the ID. About seven o'clock, in the dark, with the help of an atlas, I drove around searching for the address. It was a ground floor apartment complex with the apartment number toward the back in a darkened corner. I rang the doorbell. A young man answered and described the wallet and its contents to my satisfaction. He took the wallet, retrieved a five dollar bill and gave it to me saying "Thank you." I shudder now to think that I put myself into this type of situation and that Don went along with it. I applied the five dollars toward the purchase of a Bible from a Catholic Book Store.

Socially Challenged

A notice came in the mail from a pawn shop stating that the balance was paid in full. When I asked Don about it I learned that the money I brought into marriage and used to open a joint account, leaving the savings account record book in the glove compartment of the car, was having ten dollars a month withdrawn from it and Don was paying off my wide band wedding ring with three diamonds without my knowing about it. I liked my ring, though this payment arrangement stymied me. What else didn't I know about this man? I learned that the ring cost seventy-five dollars and he repaid it in ten-dollar installments for ten months. That was not my kind of approach to finances. Actually, I hadn't lived on my own to learn what my approach to finances might be.

Again this summer Don would have to leave for two weeks of Army Reserve Camp. The checking account balance appeared to be enough for the baby and me to survive for the two weeks. In the middle of the second week checks were beginning to bounce. With no word from Don since he left ten days earlier, I called the bank and apparently Don had been to San Francisco and cashed checks. There were two overdrawn check fees of five dollars each. How was I going to buy milk for the baby? I did not want to ask anyone for a loan.

I pulled out the phone book, checked the yellow pages for a bridal rental shop in the area and found one in Beverly Hills. I dressed up my little guy, packed up my wedding dress and veil, laid the baby on the front seat of the car that had no seat belts and headed to Beverly Hills. The store owner agreed to take only the veil and paid me ten dollars. Don returned on Saturday with more financial bad news. He had stood his army rifle up against an army truck and the truck backed over it. Don was responsible for replacing it. The cost came out of whatever check he was to receive from the military.

I don't recall how we got out of that bind. Maybe I don't want to know. How could I be upset? I was happy to see him and he brought me a sterling necklace and earrings with pearl insets. RJ got a blue stuffed dachshund with black button eyes for display, not play. We placed it in his crib for a photo option before his mother set it on the dresser.

October fifth I was scheduled for repair surgery for damage caused during childbirth. Each month since delivery we received a bill for twenty-five dollars from the anesthetist requesting payment. I broke down in tears and explained that I was scheduled the next day for delivery-related surgery. He was so gentle trying to calm me and asked that when possible I send him five dollars a month until paid in full.

That evening Don and I talked for the first time in depth about finances. I grew up in a family where Dad paid the bills and Don was accustomed to his mother paying the bills. Together we agreed that from that day forward he would keep a certain amount out of his weekly check and deposit the rest and I would be the family finance person. More issues arose and we were maturing in our communication and working through issues together.

Socially Challenged

The doctor that delivered RJ apologized for the tearing and scarring that resulted from the episiotomy at delivery, and said that he and another doctor from Santa Monica Community Hospital would accept only what insurance would pay and there would be no charge to me.

Don and I had gone a little further sexually than planned a few days earlier. I believed there was a possibility that I could have conceived but there was no way of knowing. When working at the Browerville Hospital and during the fifties there was an attitude that doctors, priests and other educated people were busy people and we didn't change their schedules. I, in my brown dress, reluctantly climbed the steps to Santa Monica City Hospital and was admitted.

Lying on the gurney awaiting surgery I told the surgeon, whom I hand never met, that there was a slight possibility that I was pregnant and please do only the scar repair and no D&C. He, in what I considered a patronizing manner, patted me on the shoulder. I was released from the hospital the next day and stayed with the Fauchers. RJ was being cared for by Aunt Claire. Don brought him home a few days later, after work.

From what I could determine no external repair work had been done to the scarred area. The general practice at the time was that doctor's charges would be sent to the patient and the patient would be responsible for forwarding the claim to the insurance company. I was appalled to read on the billing statement that the only procedure that had been performed was a D&C.

Millie Hoelscher Moran

    I suffered from depression that fall, likely attributed to both the procedure and our challenging finances. It took me awhile to admit that yes, I was angry with the surgeon and I was also angry with myself. I grew to realize that it was not the doctor who deserved all the blame. Don and I had intercourse at fertile time and may or may not have conceived. I could have been assertive enough to postpone the surgery until I was comfortable enough to move forward doing so. At any rate Don and I became more aware for the need of improved communication and to advocate for our self.

    At Christmas time we were making plans for a trip to Minnesota the following summer. RJ received a not-so-safe fun car seat from Santa that could be hooked over the front backrest of the car so RJ could see out over the dash for the four thousand mile roundtrip the upcoming June. My youngest brother, Mark, was born in February when RJ was nine months old.

    Limiting family size for selfish reasons was something frowned upon in Christian teaching. Selfish reasons meant different values for different couples. We had the conversations that if we could afford a trip to Minnesota we could also be open to a sibling for RJ. In February, I conceived and was spotting as travel plans drew near. Doctor Sumption said he believed I needed to get back to family and to continue making travel plans. He cautioned me to lie down in the back seat as much as possible, get out and walk often and unfasten the waistband buttons on clothing. The bleeding ceased.

Socially Challenged

Don sold the 1946 Ford and purchased a white 1957 Pontiac two-door Star Chief for the journey. He built a wooden platform to fit between the back and front seats for RJ to sleep on. He also placed an ad in the Los Angeles Times for someone to help drive and pay half of the gas. Dave was from Minnesota, and like many at the time, he ventured to Southern California in pursuit of the good life. He found a job and wanted to return to Minnesota to bring his wife and three boys to live in Southern California.

Dave negotiated terms that would allow for him to stop for one hour in Las Vegas to gamble. At one o'clock Saturday morning we stopped in the city that never sleeps. We waited in the car, unable to justify losing hard-earned money intended for the trip. Our thirteen-month-old couldn't sleep for all of the lights and noise on the Strip. Dave's one hour turned into two hours. We continued on.

Saturday night we stayed in a huge house-type motel and shared a bathroom with other renters. The next morning Don and I found a church for mass while Dave chose to take RJ to breakfast at a restaurant. We trusted the guy. He returned at the designated time shaking his head and probably missing his own boys. He related how RJ, wearing a white hoodie, was sitting in a highchair patiently chewing on the drawstring from his hoodie. As Dave began pulling he discovered that RJ had a foot or more of string from the hood in his mouth. Then we learned that our little trooper consumed all three pancakes that Dave had ordered for him, a surprise to Dave maybe, but not to us.

The rest of the trip was uneventful except for the four a.m. stop when I got out of the car with my skirt unfastened as the doctor ordered and the skirt fell to my ankles. Rather than going directly home, we needed to get Dave to an agreed-upon destination. We were so excited to introduce our pride and joy to our families. RJ was my parent's first and only grandchild at the time.

Chapter Twenty-three

As we approached the farm yard that we left nearly two years earlier, I gasped in shock. The house seemed so much smaller than I had remembered. The distance from the mailbox at the end of the driveway to the house appeared to be a mere dozen breaths. Back in the cold winters the steam from our nostrils for that jaunt blocked a person's view. It was treacherous. The garage and outbuildings seemed so close to each other. The environment that I grew up in seemed to have shrunk. It felt claustrophobic inside the house. While I still referred to it as home, it never again felt like home.

Siblings stared at us and we gazed back at them. RJ clung to me as my mom reached for him. How could a thirteen-month-old take it all in? I, four months pregnant, was exhausted. Siblings I recognized had grown and changed. The two new blonde brothers, four months and twenty-two months, were foreign to me. Mom had sent a few photos. My heart was heavy. I had missed out on something so much a part of me and now I was immersed into a new and more personal life. I wondered if a nine-day vacation shared with both of our families would do justice to the ache for family. We were all different and couldn't go back to former emotions. Identifying the new sensation seemed draining.

The first night in a lumpy saggy bed, my former bedroom, with RJ in a playpen next to us, we tried to get some sleep. The humidity was much higher in Minnesota than I had remembered. Sleep was a challenge. The next day we went through the same reacquainting efforts with Don's family. My little brothers were tow heads, RJ was medium blonde and Don's thirteen-month-old brother had jet black hair. With seventy-five percent fewer people in the house, RJ seemed to be able to warm up to this same age uncle, Tim, with greater ease than all of the people at the farm. I was numb.

The rest of the vacation was filled with two family reunions, two weddings and some garden fresh strawberries, rhubarb desserts and numerous early vegetables. It was important to visit with grandparents and have four generation pictures taken. Taking RJ to Saint John's for former co-workers to greet him was a favorite time. There was less chaos at the hospital than at either of our homes though the atmosphere there had transformed, too. Every one of us had our own lives. It was a hard-work vacation and the time was coming for goodbyes.

Mom took me aside for what seemed a desired mother/daughter conversation. She wanted to get a sense of "was I happy in my new life." I assured her that "yes," I was, and was looking forward to getting back home to which she responded that it hurt her to hear that I was ready to leave.

Socially Challenged

During our alone time I thanked her for how open she had with me in striving to prepare me for marriage and the marriage relationship. I went on to inform her that I didn't remember her telling me about the bleeding that can occur on the wedding night. She asked what I meant and then explained that she was menstruating for her wedding so wasn't aware of the bleeding I had identified. We hugged and I encouraged her to please tell my sisters what to expect at an appropriate age.

The following morning at six o'clock, with older brothers in the barn doing chores and the younger siblings still sleeping, Mom and Dad alone stood at the east side of the house near our vehicle as our little family got ourselves settled in for the trip back home. I turned to them and asked that they please pray for me in November. I was concerned about going into a second birth after the trauma with the first delivery plus my titer counts were being monitored for indications that my Rh negative and Don's Rh positive blood factors could cause incompatibility problems with this baby. Dad responded; "We pray for you always."

I crawled into the car sobbing and couldn't look back. Separation anxiety had taken hold of me, similar to my first weeks of school as a first grader. I curled up on the front seat and laid my head on Don's lap until we got to Willmar. Don tried to comfort me to no avail. I sat up though the tears continued until the Dakota border. At that moment it was as if I was given the gift of composure to move forward with the life that awaited us.

RJ's former calm demeanor was now totally fretful. He, who prior to leaving California could be left with a few friends or relatives without a fuss, now demanded that a parent be with him at all times. In addition he contracted the bug his Uncle Tim had a few days earlier. Several cloth diapers a day had to be discarded. It was a nightmare and concern for RJ's welfare was taking its toll.

One headache was lifted for the return trip. Don's Dad slipped Don two twenty dollar bills, to help pay for gas. We reached Culver City with only seven dollars to our name. Food was minimal for the next week until payday. When we got our feet back on the ground we reimbursed Don's parent's with twenty-five of the forty dollars. They were still feeding many mouths. We wanted them to know we appreciated their generosity yet respected their financial situation as well.

Now it was time to focus on my prenatal care, Don going for another two weeks of Army Reserve Camp and getting our finances to the point of dreaming for a house of our own. With a second baby on the way our landlady had increased our rent.

My widowed godfather/grandfather had four other such relationships with oldest children in his children's families. Shortly after Grandma passed away Grandpa gave each of these four grandchildren a twenty-five dollar war bond, which meant his original investment on each was seventeen-fifty that would mature in ten years. Mine matured when I was seventeen.

I had no use for it so I left it invested to earn a higher return. Now it was time to retrieve it from Uncle Sam and open a savings account of my own to use as I saw fit. With the combined war bond funds and the nearly thirty dollar stash I was able to open an account at the bank in the nearby shopping center in the amount of seventy-eight dollars. I was disciplined and found no need to withdraw cash from the account. Don didn't know about the growing account.

We had matured so much since having our first baby. Baby number two was a few days overdue. It was the Saturday after Thanksgiving. Contractions started and were moving along. I took aspirin for the discomfort. My titer counts had climbed though the doctor thought we could get through this birth without blood exchanges to the baby. I was frightened and had a false sense of keeping the baby in me would mean everything would be okay. I knew better but didn't want to deal with reality. I was trying to keep occupied.

Don's newly high school-graduated sister, Jean, from Minnesota, came out to assist us during this time. RJ was napping and Don was due home soon from his Saturday half-day of work. A murder had occurred at a local bar the night before and law enforcement people were searching for evidence on the railroad tracks between Culver Boulevard. I perched myself on the top step leading to the apartment where I could watch the activity.

Near midnight we left for the hospital. For days reality went blank for me. I knew that this time I wanted a private room; no more seven-bed wards. Labor or perhaps medication left me nauseated. I have no recollection of Kelly's birth. I only remember that I arrived at the hospital in the dark and now it was daylight. I felt my belly time and again and it was flatter than when I arrived. What had happened to the baby? Where was Don?

I asked nurses about the baby and never got a clear answer. One did tell me that someone would bring the baby out soon. Still there was no sign of Don. Eventually, after I don't know how long, a beautiful dark-haired girl in a pink blanket was placed in my arms. I blocked out so much. I remember Don telling me that he was embarrassed when the nurse asked me if I had any other girls and I said "Yes, one, she is thirteen years old." Apparently I was referring to my oldest sister. Don said after that he went home to get some sleep.

Again only husbands and the mother were allowed to visit. This time Roland took the initiate to visit with Don. The hospital allowed him in. Kelly jaundiced. The bilirubin count was climbing and I was informed that for precautionary measures she would be kept in the nursery. I could not hold her or breastfeed her. I took the St. Gerard (patron of mothers and babies) medal I was wearing and asked a nurse to tape it to the bassinet. Two days later I was discharged, planning to leave the baby. I don't remember taking her home, though they must have decided to discharge her with me.

Socially Challenged

A Christmas tree lot had trees discounted on December 23. I got a sad-looking specimen for seventy five cents. Christmas gifts were few to none. Both of the children had severe diarrhea Christmas Day. I went to 6 a.m. mass so Don and Jean could go later. How I longed for family to see our beautiful children. When I went to communion a tear rolled down my check onto the communion paten. "Thank you, God, for the Faucher family who invited us for Christmas dinner."

Chapter Twenty-four

1962 brought many changes to our little family. Our minds and hearts focused on the purchase of a home, but where? Real estate costs in Culver City and the surrounding area far exceeded our means. A radio commercial advertising Sun Ray Estates in Baldwin Park captured our interest. One Sunday afternoon our brood traveled through Los Angeles to San Gabriel Valley and investigated the surroundings of what could become our future home. We located the Sun Ray model home/office and retrieved information on two floor plans and costs. The next weekend Aunt Claire and Uncle Mike accompanied us to perhaps guide us through information we didn't understand. While I remember no advice from them, we signed a contract.

The unfinished house with three bedrooms a bath-and-a-half and an attached two-car garage would be ready for move in by the first of March. The cost was $14,395.00 with a down payment of $395.00 and a $2000.00 second mortgage with an interest-only monthly payment of twenty-seven dollars. The second mortgage balloon was to be paid off in five years. My savings account in Culver City had climbed to ninety-eight dollars. Add to this our income tax return and we had the down payment secured.

We gave notice on our apartment even though the carpeting was not laid in the house's living room, three bedrooms, closets and hall. Beds were set up in the new house on cement floor Saturday, March 3, and the following Tuesday we transferred everything except the kitchen table to the garage so the carpet installers could do their job.

There were twenty-seven houses in the division and we were the first to move in, which meant I was concerned being alone in the parched basin with no phone and no one to rely on for support. Don drove into LA six days a week for work and the following Sunday he had Army Reserve duty all day. I, like many women, was for the most part a single mom striving to set down roots in a new community.

Gradually more home owners took possession of their purchases. We joined St. John the Baptist Church in Baldwin Park, Don joined the Knights of Columbus and I the Parish Council of Catholic Women. A neighborhood grocery store was across the freeway. With a baby and a toddler tucked into single stroller we crossed a bridge over the freeway to the store for bread and milk. To get to Baldwin Park's Well Baby Clinic once a month I took babies and stroller on a bus into downtown, always proud of having faced my fears and the fact that somebody must be watching out for us.

****

Millie Hoelscher Moran

Following ourselves to be convinced by a door-to-door salesperson that a flagstone patio with a built in barbecue would be a good investment for our family's relaxation, we signed a contract for twenty-four monthly payments. At my design and request a metal sleeve was cemented into the flagstone floor for a collapsible clothesline to be inserted. The installers worked well with me. Both the patio and the clothesline were new concepts to us, though greatly functional and enjoyable investments.

Next we added payments for a new washer and dryer. Then we invested in window coverings. The sense of being on display for the world to see had to be eliminated. How we ever justified these purchases, I don't know. Don was working hard and making extra money. We were never late on a payment.

A few days following the delivery of the laundry appliances, I laid four-month-old Kelly on the washer, turned toward the adjacent half-bath to retrieve the floor scales to weigh myself first and then pick up Kelly and step on the scales to get an estimated weight for her. Before even picking up the scales I heard a thud and scream. Kelly had rolled over and fallen from the washer top to the hard cement floor. I was not aware that my little cutie could roll from her back to her tummy. I picked her up and we cried together.

Our Catholic understanding regarding spacing the birth of children was that this was a sacred privilege and responsibility. Children were gifts from God and we needed to discipline ourselves sexually to be able to provide for those children, while avoiding self-centered materialistic reasons for birth spacing. Jointly we came to the conclusion that if we could afford a house we could afford another baby.

It was the week between Palm Sunday and Easter. I assumed that I was burning a small piece of old palm that I found on the carpet. My period wasn't happening. I hoped that all of the excitement of a new home and adjustments perhaps threw my cycle off. While burning the palm, I was praying, asking God that perhaps a little more time would be given to us before a next pregnancy, when RJ came waltzing through the kitchen wearing a huge floppy straw hat that someone had purchased in Tijuana and given to him. I burst into laughter, blew out the burning flame and realized it wasn't a palm I was burning. God and I laughed together and, yes, baby number three was on the way.

Settling in to a more glamorous-than-apartment-living family lifestyle suddenly took an expanded dimension. Beauty Seat Covers, where Don worked, had two locations, the one on Pico Boulevard in LA and the other in North Hollywood. Don was offered the shop foreman position in North Hollywood, which meant twenty-six miles one way each day and an increase in pay. It also meant he would leave home at six a.m. while the children were sleeping and return at nine p.m. when they were again asleep.

To avoid the parking lot-type traffic conditions on San Bernardino Freeway at rush hour, he chose to work late every night and build headliners to earn twenty dollars extra per headliner. One night a week fellow employees stayed late for a game of poker. The children would see him only on weekends. Don's model car hobby turned into a real life 1948 Ford Coupe that he could drive to work. I needed our Pontiac for transporting our growing family to routine everyday activities.

****

An air mail stamped letter arrived in August, possibly indicating sad news. Mom's dad had passed away. I was told that a small heart-shaped pillow with four roses representing the four great-grandchildren on it included my two children. I was thinking there should have been a half rose for my unborn baby. We hadn't told our families of this third pregnancy yet.

To save money we refrained from having a phone installed. Once when my mother had surgery we called home from a pay phone. Rarely did I use a neighbor's phone, perhaps to make a doctor appointment. Once I needed her phone book to determine what part of the LA area the PL prefix phone number area was located. In those days letters were used rather than digits for the first two of seven numbers like PLymouth or HUboldt, followed by five numbers. I got the information that I needed for an inner city retreat event and decided not to pursue driving myself into that area.

Summer passed quickly. We got word that Don's parents were coming from Minnesota to visit us in October. With hopes of making another trip to Minnesota the following summer we had chosen to surprise our families with a six-month-old baby. We planned to have a phone installed before the arrival of the newborn. Now it was urgent for me to tell my parents about the pregnancy before the in-laws arrived. We survived seven months without a phone. A phone was installed and the urgent phone call made. When Don's mother saw me, she questioned if we had told her of the pregnancy. No, we hadn't. SURPRISE!

Also in October, the Cuban Missile Crisis sent people scurrying to grocery stores to stock up on food. Grocery shelves were bare. Our funds were limited. I didn't stock up. Thank goodness President Kennedy's handling of the situation led to tensions easing. Don was to have been discharged from the Reserves at that time though was extended a year with the possibility of being called to active duty at anytime. Blessed with a calm that allowed me to focus on the business at hand which included driving weekly into LA taking Kelly to Children's Hospital, I managed to live for each day.

Kelly had severe club feet and required casts from the knees down, to be changed weekly. A bar separated her legs. She was so good about her situation and managed to crawl, clop-clop around the house without fussing. The night before her doctor visit I'd remove the bar and place her into her jump seat with feet dangling into a container of warm vinegar water to dissolve the cast material. The casts were eventually replaced with tarso-pronator shoes shortly before the arrival of baby number three. As soon as Kelly got into shoes she started walking.

Millie Hoelscher Moran

It was the middle of December. Christmas shopping was minimal. Mom sent a naked used rubber doll out for Kelly. I sewed doll clothes. The Fauchers gave her a new doll but I stored it away in anticipation that it would be a great gift for her the following Christmas. On Saturday, December 22, with the Christmas tree half decorated, I went into labor. Don was already at work out in North Hollywood. I called him and indicated that I was having significant labor pains. When I hung up the phone a contraction which stopped me in my tracks told me to call the Love's next door to ask if they would consider driving me to the hospital if needed.

I had no experience with my pregnancies of membranes rupturing spontaneously; the doctor always preformed the pressure relieving procedure just prior to delivery and this time would be no different. To my pleasant surprise, and without me requesting, Don came home earlier than I expected. His maturity level since the first child had elevated to an informed husband and father degree. We left for the hospital immediately. Walking through the parking spot marked CHAPLAIN in the hospital's parking lot a bearing down contraction hit me and I commented, "This one is going to be a priest."

Baby Lee, named after Aunt Claire and Uncle Mike's thirteen-year-old son who died of leukemia, arrived at Queen of the Valley Hospital in West Covina minutes after getting to labor and delivery. Doctor Gore, father of seven children, delivered Lee and then left for the holidays. I was told that one of his pediatricians would check on our Rh baby. Neither Doctor Gore nor I realized that the pediatrician had not yet been approved as an on-staff doctor at the new hospital and therefore was only allowed to peer through the nursery window and ask pertinent questions of nursery nurses.

A friend of mine was also a post-partum patient. Rose was dumbfounded when informed that I called my mother with my baby news and Mom told me over her party line, "Millie, I am, too." I knew she meant that at age forty-six she was pregnant again.

I was discharged December 24. The baby was kept in the hospital until after Christmas. His bilirubin stabilized. Thank goodness he did not require blood exchanges. His jaundiced face, with gentian violet lips to prevent him from getting my yeast infection, showing out of a giant red Santa stocking provided by the hospital auxiliary was a sight to behold. Frequent trips back to the hospital lab the next week for puncturing Lee's heels for blood work kept me busy. We paid a thirteen-year-old girl, oldest of nine children, to help with my children. I had to let her go for spending so much time on the phone. It was as if I had four children in the house. Somehow we managed.

Five weeks later both Lee and Kelly came down with pneumonia. Lee was hospitalized along with five thousand other infants throughout Los Angeles County. Again it was a fretful time. Doctors were prepared to do a tracheotomy on Lee. We had to leave him at the hospital because of the sick fifteen-month-old at home. Upon arriving at home we received a call from Doctor Gore; the hospital hadn't taken insurance information from us and without it Lee would have to be sent to County General in Los Angeles. Don rushed back to the hospital with his insurance card. I called the hospital the next day to inquire about Lee's status. He was receiving antibiotics and breathing better but I didn't get back to see my cutie for two days.

When I did walk into his room and bent over his bassinet with the St. Gerard medal taped to it and said a few words to him, Lee gave me such a precious smile. I was so relieved but we weren't out of the woods yet. After Lee was discharged, diarrhea nearly took his life. He was down to below birth weight. Finally it was determined that the antibiotic killed off the necessary bacteria in his digestive tract and unpasteurized bacteria-cultured milk from Altadena Dairy, on the other side of town, would be required to get the necessary bacteria back into his intestines. Within an hour of drinking a few ounces of the milk his liquid stools were beginning to form.

The next year we were plagued with measles and ringworm on the children's scalps leaving them with bald spots that treatment rapidly resolved. We refrained from traveling to Minnesota the next summer. Mom was due in mid-summer. Six a.m., California time, on June 27, the phone rang. It was Dad telling me Mom had the baby. No airmail stamps this time. When I asked Dad the sex of the baby he wanted me to guess. I was concerned for Mom's welfare though went along with his antics and responded; "A boy?" Dad said;

"Guess again." To which I responded, "A girl?" A third time Dad asked me to guess. Exasperated I indicated it was time to be serious. Apparently no one, the doctor included, realized that two babies rested in utero. Healthy seven-pound twin girls, Peggy and Patty, shocked family and friends and I wasn't going to have take a leave of absence for these sibling births.

The beginning of the 1963, I had heard or seen bank advertisements for opening a Christmas Club account. I believed I could save five dollars out of each weeks paycheck and set it aside in the specially designated account that earned interest. For the most part 1963 was an upbeat year with our life and with the families back in Minnesota until November 22, when the world turned upside down following the death of President Kennedy. Raylene, from across the street, rushed over to tell me to turn on the television. I was glued to the images and cried often with all of the country for the next few days. Making phone calls were impossible, the circuits were jammed. I couldn't even call Don for support.

The Christmas Club account that year allowed for the children to receive a few more gifts. Our tradition was to bundle up and drive around looking at Christmas lights in upscale neighborhoods. We had no snow but we had colorful lights and entire cul-de-sac streets with life-sized decorations on their lawns.

Another tradition was added. Mr. and Mrs. Love, our next door neighbors, would stop by for gift opening and baked goods. Kelly was begging for a Tiny

Millie Hoelscher Moran

Tears doll as advertised on TV. When she opened her gift, the no-name doll from the Fauchers the previous year, she exclaimed; "My Tiny Tears doll!" I also sewed a coat and jumper for her. Kelly claimed Lee's xylophone and Lee enjoyed chewing on wrapping paper and ribbons. RJ got a gun and holster like the neighborhood boys had, and a drum, that after a few days passed, I needed a break from and put the drum on a high shelf in the closet. RJ asked; "If Santa Claus knew the drum was too noisy, why did he give it to me?" Each of the purchased toys was purchased at an eighty-eight cent sale.

All five of us received clothes suitable for an intended summer trip back home, our second in five years. My parents had not yet been introduced to Kelly or Lee and the twins, Patty and Peggy had no idea I existed. I sewed matching two-piece green and white outfits for my littlest sisters.

Chapter Twenty-five

*I*nvolvement in the parish's Council of Catholic Women organization led to my being elected the president of that organization. Feeling ill equipped for the role I decided to accept, with the assurance by others that together we could get the job done. I viewed it as taking another step to gaining confidence while serving a cause I believed in. In one of the perks of the position, the diocese had sponsored Maria Von Trapp as a guest entertainer for the hundreds of diocesan women attending a conference at LA's Ambassador Hotel. The roundish robust Maria, older than the character in the Trapp family book or movie with Julie Andrews as Maria, left me befuddled. However, her singing voice caused the pillars inside the ballroom to vibrate. It was a privilege to actually see her and shake the hand of the woman I had held on a pedestal for two decades.

That spring I went on my first silent weekend retreat at a monastery in Alhambra. Don parented so I could have much-needed alone time.

****

We started shopping for a vehicle to get us to Minnesota in June. Our one and only new car ever was a 1963 Mercury Comet station wagon. Don sewed a four-inch pad for the back which would be our hotel room for going across country. Eighteen-year-old cousin Sherry agreed to travel with us to help drive and spend time with her Minnesota cousins. Lee, a year-and-a-half old, was doing well with potty training. We actually saved a pea can and removed the label for him to use in the car if necessary. Don nailed two short pieces of two-by-four wood together to carry into public restrooms for Lee to stand on. Both inventions worked well.

Knowing there would be two large family reunions I sewed matching outfits for myself and the children, navy skirts for Kelly and me and shorts for the boys. The tops were light blue and white cotton checked. It would be easier to keep track of the children in the crowds, I thought. I used other items of clothing as patterns with a few added creative accents. I had never used a purchased pattern.

****

*M*om tried again during this visit home for a mother/daughter talk, this time about the Catholic Church teaching that it might be okay to use the newly released birth control pill for pregnancy problems. I had not ovulated in a couple of months and tired easily. At every house I visited in Minnesota I requested a bowl of ice chips. I craved ice chips. Upon returning to California I went to the doctor requesting to have my hemoglobin checked. It was at six and later dropped to four.

    I was hospitalized with blood transfusions and testing started. The day after the first two units of blood, I ovulated. The doctor said I didn't have enough blood in me for normal fertility functions. I learned that the ice chip craving could be a symptom of low hemoglobin. Multiple tests were performed with a diagnosis of severe anemia, cause unknown.

    Doctor questioned my family's roots and origin and asked if my grandparents came from the Mediterranean area. Pernicious anemia was suspected. I was trained how to give myself injections of vitamin B12 in the upper thigh once a day. Frequent testing of my hemoglobin followed and arrangements were made for me to be admitted to the City of Hope Blood and Cancer Research Center in Duarte. Prior to being admitted and following another routine blood test, my hemoglobin had jumped a couple of levels and continued to do so. The B12 injections were decreased and eventually discontinued. I never was admitted to the research center.

    The scare was enough for Don and me to have a conversation, with me encouraging him to find a good mother for the children, if I should die. We decided to arrange for a professional photographer to photograph our family. It was important to do so as a precaution if any of us would slip away.

    I had lost significant amount of weight and appeared gaunt in the photos and felt compelled to slow down my life. My health gradually returned and we took the children to the San Diego Zoo. Life was stabilizing.

****

*D*on had what I considered a most attractive smile. He avoided going to the dentist and like many in that era, decided to get dentures rather than visit the dentist regularly. We knew of someone who received dentures as a high school graduation gift. Don was twenty-five years old when he had his own teeth replaced. My heart sank the first time I saw Don with his dentures. The smile I loved was gone forever. It felt like buyer's remorse.

Antibiotic injections were ordered for Don. Our doctor said, "Millie, we know you can give injections so if you two are in agreement I will write a prescription." The nurse chimed in with; "He doesn't have much fat on him so be sure to visually section the buttock into fourths and inject into the upper outside quadrant. All went well. Don was able to keep working.

****

*O*ne of the neighbors in our twenty-seven home cul-de-sac presented to the rest of us the idea of a baby-sitting exchange. Seven of us signed on for this system, using points rather than money. Each of us started with fifty points. Points were charged for number of children and hours. We took turns being the secretary. The group arrangement worked for a year.

For neighborhood activities I, inspired by my large family status, organized neighborhood events for mothers and children. One day I called mothers of young children to invite them to meet at my house at 11:00 a.m. for a parade. Entrants were to use their imaginations as to what they wanted to do or be in the parade. Marchers clanged and banged pots and pans, pushed buggies, used clothespins to hold playing cards in place on bikes so spokes would hit the cards and send sound through the neighborhood. Mothers pulled toddlers in wagons and brought cookies or crackers for munchies. I provided Kool-Aid. The event was a big hit, except for the middle-aged man who worked nights.

Our visits with the Fauchers diminished. They were always so generous to us. One time they dropped in at our house unexpectedly and we felt privileged that we had the opportunity to host them. Don invited Mr. Faucher to go with him to the grocery store to purchase steaks for grilling. After they left for the market I spotted Don's wallet on the sofa. He returned a bit embarrassed by reaching the checkout stand before noticing his faux pas and resorted to asking our guest for a loan.

Another time Mrs. Faucher was riding in the car with me on a Sunday afternoon. Spotting something approximately a foot high, taut across the road in front of the car, I slammed on the brake. My passenger slid off the seat and under the dash tearing a hole in her nylon stocking. Her knee was gashed and bleeding. A couple of youngsters had stretched a string connected to tin cans across the street and hid in bushes on each side of the street.

Our entertainment was primarily with the Knights of Columbus families. While attending a pool party at the Palanski home in the summer of 1965, conversation focused on the red sky over Los Angeles. Our questions revolved around wondering what impact the Watts Riots and fires might have on us and our families. The rioting calmed after a few days. The evening with the red skies over Los Angeles was my brother Harry's wedding day. We were missing special events in both families.

Don had enough of driving to North Hollywood every day for work and secured a job at Acme Top Shop on Ramona Boulevard in Baldwin Park. In time he added a second job with Bill's Fleet Service. He drove an oversized van outfitted with a sewing machine and necessary equipment to do upholstery work for utility company trucks throughout a five-county Southern California area. He was putting in long days. Eventually Joe, the owner of Acme Top Shop, offered Don a partnership in the business. That worked well for a number of reasons, one being that the children, as they got older, could spend time at the shop with their dad. For entertainment they crawled around on large bolts of fabric. Their dad bought them treats from the lunch truck that came to the shop each day. Some days I filled in for Joe's wife in the office.

At the park one day I observed a group of women and children in organized activity. I learned that it was a parenting class sponsored by Baldwin Park's Adult Education Program. The next school semester I signed up with all three children. The teacher would give a presentation to mothers each week. Her assistant supervised the children. Mothers recorded observations of their children to which the teacher commented in red pencil for moms to learn from the following week.

The book used was from Gesell Institute's parenting series. I learned so much. I was sad the day I spoke up in the parenting group and stated that I am not sure I love my children. I longed for the best for each of them but it seemed so much like the responsibility, the charges I had at home with siblings. The teacher suggested that I tell the children many times a day that I loved them and chances were that eventually I would believe it. I wasn't sure what love was. That was my next lesson. I did love them.

In addition to learning the psychology of child development and behavior, I came away with very practical and welcomed information about life from sources beyond the Catholic Tradition. Something that I cherish today is a no name recipe that one of the moms shared that children supposedly would love. The verbal directions were to peel and boil a few potatoes. While potatoes boiled, turn oven to 350 degrees. Brown chopped onion and a pound of ground beef. Add a can of drained green beans and one can of Campbell's tomato soup. Add one-half tomato can of milk to the mixture. Set meat mixture aside. Mash the cooked potatoes. Spread potatoes over warm meat mixture. Sprinkle top with grated cheese of choice (usually

Velveeta or Cheddar). Place in oven until cheese is melted and slightly browned. My family requested the casserole often.

At the same time, my friend Barb, a mother of four girls, invited us to her high school graduation party. She informed me about the GED program that was for people who dropped out of high school, usually after two years, and was originally intended for military people. While I had never attended high school, I inquired and learned that this was my chance. I could take the GED test and then attend classes for however long it took for me to meet academic requirements.

My life had freed up enough that I could justify starting school and work around Don's and my schedules. I chose neighboring El Monte High School to begin with because of classes I wanted or needed that were available at times conducive to my goals. In addition to classes at EMHS, I eventually took a typing class in Alhambra, algebra in West Covina, history, math and medical terminology in Covina and the GED test back at El Monte.

I was thrilled when the teacher that facilitated the testing process was giving back test results. Each of three young men ahead of me was informed that they would have to retake the test. I prepared myself to remain composed if I received the same sentence. I nearly lost that composure when he said; "Mildred, you did very well." (No score given.) "Congratulations!" Two years of classes were eliminated by the test. I probably broke a Guinness Book of Records record, not because

Socially Challenged

I passed the test in my first attempt but because I became pregnant with my fourth child in my first month of taking classes for credit.

****

*B*aby Jennie arrived on March 18, 1967. She required two blood exchanges. The hospital absorbed some of the costs incurred that the insurance didn't cover. I had talked to our pastor during the pregnancy about my financial concern. We never saw a hospital bill. For this baby we could finally justify buying a rocking chair. Don found a used maple rocker in the want ads and he sewed new cushions for it, all for forty dollars. Our little pumpkin did well. Jennie was our first child that was cared for by a private practice pediatrician. No more Well Baby Clinics.

We were embedded in our community that provided family activities. RJ was old enough to join Little League Baseball. Trips to the library became more frequent. Because of our good fortune with our many blood transfusions, Don signed up for Knights of Columbus monthly blood mobiles. I was advised to refrain from doing so for health reasons.

My sister, Jeanette, who was Jennie's godmother, by proxy, flew out to visit us the summer following Jen's birth. We had wonderful sister times in Disneyland, Hollywood and the movie *Thoroughly Modern Millie*, at the hair dresser, beach and K of C dinners. Jeanette shared that she was dating Bill Somebody. It took me awhile to realize that Bill was little Billy Schoenecker, the nine-year-old in room 103 when

Millie Hoelscher Moran

I worked in the Browerville Hospital. Room 103 was on the medical ward so I didn't care for him, though I overheard the nurses at nurse's station discussing poor little Billie who had pneumonia and required so many penicillin shots that his buttocks were turning black and blue. Could this be, yet another former patient that just might become a member of the family?

With my erratic menstrual cycles, heavy bleeding and previous hemoglobin history, after talking with my doctor and pastor, Don and I decided I would try the "Pill" for a while. When in the progesterone phase of the prescription I got such severe headaches that I would be bedridden for days prior to onset of menses. The hormone pill prescription was discontinued. Some years later a lower hormone dose was again tried, and the headaches were less intense and the sexual freedom was welcomed for a few months. We dedicated ourselves to abstaining from intercourse a week mid-cycle as was a discipline associated with natural family planning. With each menstrual period we sent money to an adopted child that we supported in Africa. While on the pill and not ovulating my sexual desire planed out. That was no fun. We chose to return to a healthier lifestyle of no medical prescriptions or procedures that were contraceptive in nature. We preferred the dating/honeymoon phases of living with our fertility. Each time we made it through another cycle without a pregnancy, we sent money to the support the African child.

Don's sister and family spent a few years living in Orange County. We enjoyed having extended family time with them. When we learned that the four of them were flying to Minnesota for Christmas we decided that we would forego Christmas gifts for our family and purchased plane tickets for the same flight as theirs. Children under age four flying with an adult flew free. Children age five to twelve were half price. Our family ticket cost was reasonable.

About that time a stranger stopped by the shop and Don called home to get my opinion about using most of our savings to purchase a man's truckload of new padded dash boards, headliners and ready-made seat covers. I told him I would meet him at church so we could make a visit to the Blessed Sacrament and pray together for discernment in this regard. We decided to be risk takers. The purchase was for $350.00. The next weekend Don took a minimal amount of his newly acquired inventory to North Hollywood, his previous employer, who purchased just a small portion of the upholstery supplies for double what we had paid for it. We made it to Minnesota for Christmas with money in the bank and a nine-month-old cutie to introduce to family.

As our plane descended into the Twin Cities Airport a long joyful groan arose in unison from the passengers. It was snowing. A Santa-like voice echoed through the plane. The pilot proclaimed to one and all: "Merry Christmas!" Jenny, in a pink snowsuit sent by my mom, a hand-me-down of the twins, was our Christmas gift to family.

Jeanette accepted an engagement ring from Bill on Christmas Eve in front of the Christmas tree at our farm home, with much of the family present. Throughout my childhood and which was still the practice, Christmas gifts were left unwrapped. Most of the family would go to the barn while Santa and his helpers displayed the purchases, which Mom had stored on an upper shelf in Mom and Dad's closet, around the base of the tree. Then Santa and helpers would go to the barn as well.

After milking chores were completed we walked as a group back to the house, listening for Santa and trying to determine if the tree lights had been turned on by him. Once in the house we waited in the laundry room until all were ready to descend upon the added décor to the living room. It was always chaos. This year had a few changes to the tradition that I grew up with, but still the chaos. The children were sent upstairs to play while guys did the chores and women cleaned up after supper. At some point we advanced to the living room where mom was around the base of the tree and handing gifts in all directions to hands attached to squealing, excited little voices. Mom handed me two pair of colored women's underwear. As in childhood years, within a half hour several small toys were already broken. Later Mom pulled me aside. She asked if I would return one pair of underwear. She had forgotten a gift for Kate. Shortly thereafter I found Kate crying in the closet.

Len, who was now named Roy, the name given to him by the Capuchins, had taken up guitar. He had an excellent voice, as did many in the family. We enjoyed music. Then a tradition that I was unaware of began to happen. Roy perched himself upon a chair in front of the Christmas tree and started singing Christmas songs. The three-and-a-half-year-old twin sisters, that I couldn't tell apart, moved in toward Roy and very confidently sang out a song I had never heard before about a toy that went zip when I pulled it, bop when it stopped . . . then on to "Mary's Little Boy Child." I exited the living room and headed to Kate's crying chapel, the walk-in closet. I had missed so much from my sibling's lives and they were disconnected from mine.

The fact that we came home for Christmas meant I would not return to Minnesota the next summer for Jeanette and Bill's wedding. That was the fourth sibling wedding that I would miss due to living in California. I loved my life in California and missed my family.

Chapter Twenty-six

My brother Roy, with the Capuchin religious order, informed me that another Capuchin had an aunt and uncle living a short distance from us in El Monte. Father Danny apparently sent information to his relatives about us. With a simple phone call our lives were brought together. Mr. and Mrs. Benjert, Frank and Angie, transplants from Milwaukee, were in their sixties and we were twenty-something when our families met. The Benjerts were married before the Great Depression and tell of having a home and planning to buy a new car but delayed their plans, thinking it wisest to wait until the stock market rebound. They would have been better off having purchased the car because they lost all of their investments. Frank had been a barber in Milwaukee's Grain Exchange building and Angie a legal secretary. The Benjerts were older when they married and had no children. Our relationship became somewhat three generational. We continued to have our life, though spent time together for the holidays and various other occasions. They seemed to enjoy our children and we relished the many varieties of home-made cookies they gave us each Christmas. Their home was immaculate with Provincial-style furniture.

The Benjerts had a carpenter build a wall-to-wall enclosed, glass-cased floor-to-ceiling cabinet in their living room to display hundreds of Marian statues from around the world. Most statues were purchased on their world travels and some were gifts from family and friends. They used whatever occasion to give us Hummel figurines and collectibles. Occasionally we would be given valuable smaller tables, a beige antique hair care set and a magnifying glass used for Frank's coin collection. We were being exposed to glamorous living like never before.

Our new friends were solid Catholics and shared stories of their pride and joy, their nephew Father Danny, and especially his caring for another well-known Capuchin, a stigmatic, Padre Pio, in his declining years. Our new friends were groomed throughout life as Latin Catholics. I too, as a cradle Catholic, started in my faith tradition attending all Latin masses. The only English heard was the homilies. In the early '40's many of we Catholics understood that Latin was the universal language for celebrating mass throughout the world and that it would never change. We studied Latin, sang Latin and were told wherever we attended mass throughout the world it would seem like home. And it did.

By the late forties; rumor had it that the Church Fathers decided it was important for congregations to understand the prayers being prayed. By the early fifties Sunday missals and daily missals were printed by the millions for use in the United States as a means of easier transitioning to pending changes. Both missals had Latin readings in the left column and the English translation in the right. I was at the perfect age for memorization and thoroughly enjoyed getting a sense of being bi-lingual. As with any change, some people embraced the new approach, others left the church.

Change would move forward and slow down to allow dioceses and countries to catch up. Vatican ll (1962-1965) brought more confusion and another exodus of clergy, religious and laity. I welcomed the sense of staying centered and focused while avoiding being radical in either direction. My father's words after eighth grade, "Remember, you've learned the truths of your religion in Catholic School, now don't let other teachings sway you," had to be laid to rest or at least expanded. While the basic theological teachings never changed I found it exhilarating to pay attention to the history of the world, religion and especially the Catholic tradition.

Religion, politics, sex and drug revolutions seemed to be fighting for media headlines in the sixties. I welcomed my life's distractions. It took four years of me taking high school classes at my family's pace for me to graduate in a class of ninety- two people and I didn't know another soul. How I appreciated Don's support throughout this endeavor. My siblings Roy and Kate flew in for the graduation ceremony, at which

Lee pulled out his first tooth. I fantasized that my parents were hidden from me and would appear at the ceremony. Mom and Dad were no-shows. The family sent flowers. Friends gathered to celebrate me, something that seldom happened.

****

During this era we started camping at the beach, mountains and in Mexico, graduating from pitching a tent to a pop-up tent trailer and eventually a pickup and camper. Don invested in a mustard yellow dune buggy and he glued big flowered vinyl print to the outside of the buggy. The in-stock fabric that wasn't selling at the shop also ended up on our picnic table bench seats, a tri-fold exercise pad for me and a beach bag. I detested the appearance of the mustard color and the fabric. Don was proud of his artistic creations. The enjoyable family times associated with these repulsive designs compensated for my dislike.

My personal desire to cling to our first house that gave us seven years of memories lost out to Don's desire to move to a bigger home in more affluent West Covina. I had invested myself into every corner of our first home, and I refused to sign the sale contract in Don's presence and told the relator to call me back in a few days. He did and I sat at the kitchen table and sobbed uncontrollably before finally signing. The move to Don's more desirable location went relatively smoothly, except for Don getting kidney infection and so depressed when he had to cancel a planned camping trip.

Millie Hoelscher Moran

Life in West Covina moved into a positive dimension. With children in school we were quickly drawn to families with similar interests. Pete and Yola Kochis, parents of eight children, lived a couple of blocks away. We got word that their college-aged son was killed in a plane crash. There was a private funeral that left us at a loss as to how to reach out to the family. Like us, they had no family in the area. Yola accepted my invitation to go out to lunch. Some weeks later, Kochis family members still living at home joined us for dinner. I decided to triple the no name casserole recipe given to me by the pre-school mom back in Baldwin Park. A huge tossed salad, bread and dessert fed all of us. Don's and my large family experiences served us well in feeding this large group.

As my comfort level with Yola grew I did something I had never done before. I was driving near my house when I spotted Yola's eighth grade daughter hitch-hiking. There had been frightening news about happenings of events in the San Gabriel Foothills. I was pretty sure that Yola would not approve of her daughter's hitch-hiking. I drove over to the young lady and told her that I would wait for her mother to call me about the incident. If I hadn't heard from Yola by eight o'clock that evening, telling me her daughter's version of the story, I would call Yola and explain what I saw. By five p.m. Yola called. I was comfortable with her account of the teenager's frightening choices. Little did I know that my actions would lead to the two of us mothers becoming like sisters even though we had large families back east.

Socially Challenged

****

*O*ur summers were filled with swimming, organ lessons, baton and skating lessons, Little League baseball, softball and Scout camps. Neighborhood teenagers served as reliable babysitters. We were freer to socialize with peers. We felt comfortable allowing the children to play outdoors evenings and trick-or-treating on Halloween without our supervision. Playing pinochle with six couples that met at one another's homes monthly became a favorite pastime. The couples included Don's business partner and his wife, their neighbors and three couples from our new church and school including Pete and Yola. As families we camped in the mountains together, went snow sliding in the mountains and thirty of us gathered at an upscale restaurant for Easter Brunch one year. We were like family.

Our Knights of Columbus friends, the Rayden's, had six children, a few old enough to attend Bishop Amat High School in La Puente where we intended to someday send our children. Future pro football players Pat Haden and John McKay were fantastic high school football players. We enjoyed our Friday nights in the fall with friends at Amat's games. In addition to being a winning team the half-time performance was spectacular. The dance line had won numerous awards. Nearly one hundred and fifty girls, each carrying two flash lights, professionally choreographed, high stepped onto the field. Once in position and before the music started the stadium was darkened and flashlights lit. Early in the season the lights were school colors, as playoffs reached the holiday season, colors became green and red. State finals were played at Angel Stadium in Anaheim. Amat won!

****

California and Colorado were the first states to legalize abortion. I was considering going on to nurse's training after high school though didn't want to deal with abortion in the hospital setting. Los Angeles doctors and their wives and a few attorneys organized the Southern California Right to Life organization. I attended a few meetings and was paired up with people in the San Gabriel Valley to call attention to what abortion was and to inform students and others of pre-birth developmental stages. Four different stages of spontaneous abortion babies in jars of formaldehyde were provided to me for teaching purposes. The smallest was an eight-week-old fetus. The largest was six months, fit into a suture container. Contrary to today, in the beginning there were no fetal development teaching aids readily available in schools and elsewhere. Eventually diagrams and molded-models of babies in utero were made available to the Right to Life Speaker's Bureau.

My three most memorable speaking events were to an area Toastmasters group of about twenty men. Not a single man asked questions. Another was at high school and a tenth grade male came up after class and asked if I knew which city the twelve-week-old baby came from. His girlfriend was twelve weeks pregnant when she had an abortion. My heart ached for him. A third time a meeting was organized at our church and area doctors spoke, not all of whom were Catholic. The auditorium was filled to overflowing. This topic weighed heavily on me and after a year I chose to withdraw from the speaker's bureau.

****

That summer RJ, age ten, accompanied my sister, Kate, traveling by plane to spend the summer on the family farm in Minnesota for three months. He thoroughly enjoyed his relatives and the farm. Don was growing tired of California's bursting population, the crowds at events and congested traffic. He started researching California, Colorado Springs and Minnesota for employment or business possibilities. The following summer, with our tent trailer, we drove east. After dropping his family off, Don returned to California and work. The children and I spent six weeks parked on Mom and Dad's front lawn or in the Moran's backyard. I sent photos back to Don and he pretty much decided he was ready to live in Minnesota. Photos of lakes with no boats in the background on a holiday weekend consumed his thinking. Don joined us in July and did some job searching. He made arrangements with Sis Upholstery in St. Cloud for employment whenever he could get the family moved.

For whatever reason, Don and I thought we could return to California, sell the business and house and get moved back that same fall. Classes started earlier in Minnesota than in California so we decided to enroll the children in Browerville parochial schools, that would be on same schedule as St. Cloud parochial schools. My parents wanted us back in Minnesota so badly; they agreed to have the three oldest children, ages eleven, nine and eight live with them until our return.

We flew back to California, leaving our car and tent trailer in Minnesota. The house didn't sell as quickly as we'd hoped so Don flew back after the first quarter and report cards and drove the three kids back home and to classes at Sacred Heart School in Covina. Lee, a third grader, was a compliant — good — student. His classmates were excited by the news of his anticipated return. The young new teacher of the class refused to take Lee. Judging by the students' enthusiasm, she assumed it would be too much of a distraction. I wished I had been more assertive. Thank goodness Lee had positive relationships in the other class as well and he adjusted just fine. That was a lot to ask of our parents and children. I was so lost without the children, though curly-haired, pigtailed Jennie got quality one-on-one time from me. I also enrolled her in preschool.

The children seemed to adjust well to the bouncing around. I was active with Sacred Heart's Council of Catholic Women. At one board meeting we were informed by the Diocesan CCW that Doctors John and Lyn Billings, fertility specialists from Australia, would be speaking on the Ovulation Method of Child Spacing in the LA area. Each Diocesan parish was asked to send a representative or two to the event. I was asked to represent our parish and report back. When asking who would join me, my friend Ellie with seven children responded; "Not me, I don't even know how chicken eggs are fertilized." Laughter was so spontaneous. The subject got changed without out me telling Ellie that I, the farm girl, had observed hens and roosters doing their mating maneuvers though had no clue how eggs were actually fertilized. No one joined me in attending the conference.

I left the conference disappointed. For some reason I anticipated that the new information would give me knowledge to simplify identifying ovulation. Clear cervical mucus at fertile time wasn't news to me though the Billings information was scientifically based. Self/couple discipline and charting would still be required. The added information was helpful, though Don and I both longed for easier.

****

Throughout the winter months Don worked out an exit plan with his business partner. In the spring the house was put on the market. We had an offer and were ready to accept when, Joe, the business partner, had a heart attack and passed away. We chose to not accept the offer until we could wrap our heads around all that was happening.

Through all of this I informed Don that I was having such vivid romantic dreams of other men, including a previous pastor and Don's Knights of Columbus friends, especially one. My heart fluttered like a teenager's when in the presence of this guy. Don was making plans for a beach getaway for our two families, only the friend's wife would not be going and Don had to work but would join us for the weekend. I told Don it wasn't going to happen. He emphasized that I needed to get away and this would be our last time at the beach. I decided to tell him that I couldn't go alone with this friend, the one I was attracted to.

Don laughed out loud when he learned who my fantasy guy was and stated that he trusted the friend. I told him to forget it, I didn't trust myself. This made me realize that I needed distance from the gentleman and that the move to Minnesota was best for what I was experiencing. I learned shortly thereafter that men reach their greatest sexual peak sometime between the ages of eighteen to twenty-five and for women it was somewhere between twenty-five and forty. I learned that such infatuations are not uncommon during those greatest sexual peak phases. My thoughts and dreams were normal. I had not acted upon them. No need to feel guilty.

Chapter Twenty-seven

Of all the years of living in California, we had attended absolutely no funerals. No one that we knew had died until now. Don was asked to be a pallbearer for his business partner's funeral. He declined, explaining that he did not want to cry during the service. In our large Minnesota families children were part of wakes and funerals. I decided to take our children to the viewing, partially to prepare them for deaths in our families once we moved back to our home state. To my surprise, the four children and I were alone with the embalmed body. The funeral service was held at the mortuary with about twenty people present, quite the contrast from our pre-marriage experiences.

Getting out of California alive was not going to be easy. The partnership insurance policy affiliated with Acme Top Shop was in the custody of the deceased person's nephew, the insurance agent. There was a $10,000.00 insurance policy. Getting attorneys involved made no sense to either party. If my memory serves me correctly, the widow paid Don one dollar for Don's share in the business. The house sold and the closing was scheduled to happen as Don finished his commitment at the shop.

Garage sales, packing, storage and organizing a moving van kept me busy. Pete and Yola held a farewell party for us. I wore a long fuschia and floral dress with hot-pants that I sewed and high black boots so popular in the seventies. Yola organized a game where the name of a movie star was placed on the honored guest's backs. Don's was Tiny Tim and mine was Grace Kelly. Other guests would give clues to the two of us about our celebrity and see which of us could give the correct answer first. I won.

All of the organization and working with family members who came to assist me in driving a station wagon and a pickup with a camper back to Minnesota must have taken a toll on me. One morning, Pat Hayes, a woman from church that I rarely visited with, rang the doorbell and left a prayer card regarding the Wound on the Shoulder, Jesus' shoulder, from carrying the cross. Pat must have thought I too was appearing burdened.

Finally on July 27, thirteen years to the day that Don and I married and left Minnesota, I, my four children, my brother Gerard, who had a fractured clavicle bone and was unable to do farm work and Don's San Diego sister, her husband and daughter set out for the Midwest. Don's plan was to assist the packers with clearing out the house and garage, sell his 1956 Chevy Nomad station wagon, which he eventually nearly gave away and finished with his work at the shop.

Socially Challenged

When I reached Minnesota, I called him and learned he developed a kidney infection, just as he had when moving from our first house and had to cancel a planned camping trip in the mountains with friends. The first time he broke down and cried, so disappointed to have to change the children's plans. This time I was very concerned about my partner, whether he would get himself healthy before boarding a plane to join his family. He managed to do so.

Once back with family, the search for a community that matched our desires and a house that fit our budget began. Within a few days after his arrival, Don started working for Sis Upholstery, as agreed upon the previous summer. While living in California, we had many Minnesotan relatives visit for a week at a time. A couple even lived with us for several months. Now we were in need of lodging and welcomed offers. Don stayed with my brother's family in St. Cloud. The children and I stayed at my family's farm near Browerville.

We located and purchased a house in the country near Sartell and moved in on the first day of school. The three oldest children were enrolled at St. Francis and Jennie at Sartell Elementary for kindergarten. I dropped her off at her school in the morning the first day and the bus brought her to the new house. I was waiting for her. That was a stressful day, but came with a feeling of accomplishment. We notified Allied Moving and Storage Company in California that furniture could be delivered. It would be several days so we carried mattresses from the camper into the newly purchased house and the children slept in sleeping bags.

With children, education and extra-curricular activities requiring our attention, it didn't take long to get a system up and running. Our children made friends quickly. My heart ached the day RJ asked for suggestions for something to take to school for show and tell. When I suggested the rattles from a rattlesnake his dad had shot during a family camping trip the previous summer in the Piute Mountains in the California desert, RJ absolutely refused. He explained that Minnesota kids didn't want to her about California. He got the impression that Minnesota people thought Californians were wealthy. We didn't know any wealthy Californians. We were watching every penny.

As for our new house, the main floor kitchen area was large though cabinets had no partitions in them. We used the kitchen in the basement through the winter months until we could remodel the main floor kitchen, which turned into the following summer. A family of six had lived in the basement long before the upper level of the house was built. This was our first time ever having a basement and the basement alone was larger than our first California home.

The first snow fell on November seventh, my mom's birthday. The children were so excited they went outside and made snow angels before the bus arrived. This would be our first year that we could entertain relatives during the holidays. We decided to hold an open house on Christmas Eve day for both of our families.

Fifty plus people came to celebrate with us. Jennie received a doll for Christmas. The other children wanted a snowmobile and were willing to forego other gifts. While younger people snowmobiled the adults ate, drank, and were merry. When everyone left, Don and I were on and absolute high. We cleaned up the house and went to bed. Child number five was conceived on Christmas Eve 1972. Actually, we had talked about how we knew the risks with our Rh incompatibility situation, but longed to have a child to be spoiled by relatives.

While I knew I was pregnant, on January 23, 1973, one day after the Roe v. Wade Supreme Court decision, I went to the doctor and had my pregnancy confirmed. That evening while watching a Twin Cities television news program, explicit pictures were shown depicting the aftermath in a city operating room following a legal abortion. I cried and felt sick knowing that the fleeting thought of, "If I had an abortion, no one, not even family, would have to know that I was pregnant." Don and I would know.

There was another Moran family, no relation, in the community. They were Irish. Don's family was French. One day Nancy dropped in unannounced and introduced herself. She explained how she was going out speaking in the community about abortion and the national and local Birthright organization that offered adoption alternatives and support to women and girls experiencing pregnancy challenges. The children knew I was pregnant, though we hadn't shared our baby news with the community as yet.

Lee, from the Home and School organization at St. Francis, called to see if I would address the upcoming parent-teacher organization regarding parents and the abortion issue. How did he know my past experience of speaking on the subject? Nancy provided Minnesota abortion-related handouts. The school cafeteria was filled to capacity. I wore my new green transitional dress, not quite ready for maternity clothes that the children and I had shopped for. I did my best with presenting the information I had and got the impression that while some parents and teachers welcomed the information, others were uncomfortable with the topic. I wondered, "Did my speaking on the abortion subject create a wall between me and the locals or our family and the locals?"

Easter Sunday, during the Consecration of the Mass, I felt a flutter in my lower abdomen. As an experienced mother, I was pretty sure I felt this baby for the first time. We accepted an invitation to my parent's house for Easter dinner with the family. My brother, Allen, and his fiancé', Linda, announced that they were engaged to be married. I was excited to think that after missing so many sibling weddings, this would be a first for me. They went on to explain their plans for a late September wedding. If my pregnancy would go full term, I would miss another wedding. The dear hearts moved their wedding up a month for my benefit. Al informed me that I was a mother image to him and he felt abandoned when I got married and left home. They were going to do their best to have me at their wedding.

Socially Challenged

Linda was the little dark curly-haired girl peeking into the nursery window as mentioned in an earlier chapter. I sure appreciated their gesture.

The next few days I felt more fluttering. "Was it a boy or a girl?" So far my children's birth order was a boy, a girl, a boy, and a girl, all born on holiday weekends. Mother's Day, Thanksgiving, Christmas, and Easter which meant my physicians left town after the delivery and I and my babies were left in the hands of doctors unknown to me. Would this time be any different? Fathers were not allowed in the St. Cloud Hospital delivery room for the birth of the baby. I joined the local Le Leche International group for breast feeding support. Members encouraged Don and me to take the six week childbirth classes. The hospital's fathers in delivery policy could change before I delivered.

Even with the wedding date moved ahead, my gynecologist cringed at the thought of my traveling so close to delivery date. He advised that I climb up to the over cab bed in our camper and lie down to travel, which I did. I had a joyous time at the wedding. The doctor said nothing about dancing, so I danced.

At my doctor visit the following Friday, I was told that if I didn't go into labor by the next day, I would have to be induced. The bilirubin had dropped and that was an indication of the baby being in distress. Driving home from the clinic I had to pull the car to the side of the road for a significant contraction. I suspect my doctor may have scratched the membranes in hope of starting labor. When I got home my parents were at the house with pickles and tomatoes from their garden that Mom was determined to can immediately. So be it!

Don and I went to the hospital at two a.m. The wife of Don's Knights of Columbus insurance agent was the night supervising nurse. She allowed Don to be with me throughout the night of labor. When the day nurse came on duty, Don was shooed from my presence. I had to close this deal alone.

Frail little Keith Donald arrived prematurely, a week after the wedding, on Labor Day weekend. Don was not allowed into delivery. When on the delivery table and legs in stirrups, the anesthetist asked what he could do for me. Using information I learned in the parent education classes; my response was; "Please have a wet washcloth available for me to bite on when pushing and when I bring my shoulders up to push, please support my shoulders." He did. When the delivery process was over, the anesthetist exclaimed: "That is the way they all should be." I was proud of my accomplishment and wished Don could have been with me. We had both grown so much through our first fifteen years of marriage. It would have been the icing on the cake to experience the climaxing fruit of our love together.

Baby Keith required four blood exchanges during the first few days. One night I was awake so walked to the nursery to see how he was doing, only to learn that his pediatrician and a nurse were in a small room preforming a blood exchange on Keith. I peeked into the room. It was as if I was in a cloud looking down on the procedure that I assisted with years earlier at the Browerville Hospital. I returned to my room and calmly knelt near my bed in prayer. A nurse came to the room to talk with me. For whatever reason, I had a sense of peace even though there had been pertinent lab information that was not communicated and understood between two pediatricians. Keith's titer count was in the thirties and I was told a count that high could result in brain damage. This birth was our first experience with the Bili Light for jaundice in newborns. Keith was baptized at the hospital. My roommate was his proxy sponsor. Circumcision was delayed until a later date. Why circumcise if the baby wouldn't survive? Why cause unnecessary stress to the infant?

Contrary to California hospital visitor policy, the St. Cloud Hospital allowed for visitors who were at least sixteen years old. With Keith's delicate condition, I asked the supervising nurse if the three oldest children, ages ten, eleven and thirteen could be allowed to come up the elevator after visiting hours to view their fragile baby brother, housed under a bili light in an incubator. The nurse said it would be okay to bring six-year-old Jennie up as well. I didn't want to be too bold so chose to leave that darling six-year old alone down in the night lobby. What was I thinking? Actually, I knew the standard belief at the time was that younger children were more inclined to bring diseases into hospitals. I thought it disrespectful to other patients to push the limits.

Millie Hoelscher Moran

The first year of Keith's life he was like an appendage of his mother. I took breast feeding on demand seriously. He was a skinny little kid with a big head that concerned the pediatrician. Keith's siblings labeled him ET. Sometimes they called him Skeeter. Later his schoolmates called him Gumby. It was all worth it. As I write this, that fragile child is nearly forty years old. He still has the big German head. He is six feet two inches tall, weighs 200 pounds, has a good job, owns a house in St. Louis Park and a year ago finally married. Rachel is twenty weeks pregnant with their first child, a boy, that Keith just informed me looked like ET on the ultrasound. Technology, policy and trends have come a long way since the 1950s. So have I.

Chapter Twenty-eight

Adjusting to our new life as a family in Minnesota had its challenges. Finances were tight. In addition to Don's nine-hour-a-day job with Sis Upholstery, Don scanned the *Times* want ads and located a near-new industrial Pfaff sewing machine. Our basement laundry room allowed for a sewing table to be constructed, with a lower shelf to store rolls of upholstery fabric. Customers came from every direction, thanks to our large families, friends and word of mouth. Don put in long work days with two jobs plus managed to attend children's activities and read the newspaper, especially the headlines and want ads.

My life, with a fragile newborn and then toddler, kept me close to home. Both the St. Cloud *Times* and the Catholic St. Cloud *Visitor* carried articles regarding the Australian doctors John and Lynn Billings (who I wrote of earlier) who had headlined a conference that I attended a year earlier in Los Angeles. Apparently, the husband/wife doctor team had also been key speakers at a conference at St. John's University in Collegeville, Minnesota, and would be returning the following summer to Minnesota and St. John's.

Millie Hoelscher Moran

There was a local contact phone number listed regarding the St. Cloud Diocese Family Life Bureau. The local organization had introduced the Billing's Ovulation Method of Natural Family Planning to area churches, organizations and marriage preparation classes. Kay, the director of NFP, invited me to her office for an interview.

I agreed to attend a limited number of meetings to learn with other local employees of the organizational goals for spreading the good news throughout the diocese and beyond. Don and I became the presenters for the monthly Christian Marriage and Sexuality talks in St. Cloud, which included an introduction to fertility awareness far superior to the longtime Catholic-promoted Rhythm Method for child spacing. Thus began a seven-year affiliation as a part-time diocesan employee. In addition to the employee status and the local organization's connection to international efforts to support couples and organizations throughout the world, the greatest benefit for Don and me was the support of other couples in our own marriage.

For several years my work with couples was done over the phone, assisting in interpreting the signs they were charting. If necessary, individuals or couples would meet at the home of an instructor until it became apparent that there was a need for greater professionalism and meeting in an office setting. We core instructors met on a regular basis and with others in outlying areas on a quarterly time frame.

Socially Challenged

While the Billings Ovulation Method focused only on interpreting discharge of vaginal mucus, my background incorporated the Couple to Couple League information of Basal body temperature and cervical exam. The cervical exam required inserting the middle finger into the vagina and determining that the cervix is soft and open during fertile time and closes tightly after ovulation.

With Don and my Rh incompatibility situation, I continued to feel most comfortable with the temperature and cervical exam. During one of our core instructor meetings as I explained the cervical exam, a reregistered nurse, a wife and mother, proclaimed; "The vagina is a sterile area." In silence, the five of us exchanged puzzled glances before erupting into a group roar of laughter.

In addition to presenting in the diocese, Don and I were booked for speaking engagements in northern and western Minnesota, and as far west as Aberdeen, South Dakota. For the Aberdeen engagement the five children were accommodated at a ranch belonging to people of the community. Don and I slept at the parish rectory. We explained the dating (fertile time) and the honeymoon time of a postponing pregnancy couple's cycle and how we are able to plan vacations and life around the cycles. A gentleman in the filled-to-capacity church basement raised his hand and asked if we planned the speaking engagement around our cycle. To this we answered; "This event was scheduled on the Aberdeen's parish's time."

Millie Hoelscher Moran

Once, when returning from a speaking engagement, Don chauffeured and I was moved to write fifty questions to include in our presentation as a means of companioning the participants in their learning curve. The response was absolutely — amazingly — positive. Showing the quiz to my supervisor and the rest of the staff; the questioner's contents, with minor tweaking, became standard criteria for certifying new instructors locally and beyond.

Father Paul Marx, OSB, from St. John's Monastery traveled globally promoting fertility awareness. It was humbling to be a presenter for the related International Symposium held at St. John's University in Collegeville, Minnesota. Doctors, clergy and instructors from around the world were present. I was most intrigued by the technology used so participants could hear the presenters in their native language. For me, it was a glimpse of how communication occurred in the 1970s at United Nations meetings.

As a breastfeeding-mother with growing knowledge of how erratic a woman's menstrual cycle can become once an infant is no longer totally breastfed, I assumed the responsibility of coaching the breastfeeding mothers. The unpredictable cycles were similar for off the "Pill" and pre-menopausal women. At first I worked with all three categories, though the breastfeeding mothers soon demanded more than one instructor's focus.

Soon our organization's speaker's bureau was invited into area schools to speak to eleventh and twelfth grade family living and current event classes. The 1970s sexual revolution was upon us. If Planned Parenthood was presenting devices, the "Pill" and surgical procedure information to our young people, fertility awareness people felt compelled to emphasize the value of self-discipline and learning to be a friend long before engaging in sexual activity in a relationship. Both camps believed they were promoting what we considered the freedom to be in control of our own bodies.

We fertility awareness people would tell students that waiting with sexual activity until marriage offered so many positives for life, including preventing sexually transmitted diseases and unplanned pregnancies. My heart longed to get the message across, from personal experiences, of how harsh the "Pill" could be on a woman's endocrine system with glands secreting hormones throughout the body. Realizing that in the big picture, a young female body is still in the beginning stages of producing mature ova on a cyclic basis. The "Pill" stops or alters that process. I shuddered as to how tampering with fertility might someday lead to infertility.

This was a controversial topic. Young people seemed amazed that adults could speak respectfully about reproduction. Presenting in my own children's classes left me wondering how their peers reacted to them following my presentations. I never got the impression that it was negative. One comment from my daughter was that a friend told her that when shopping with her mother, prior to a mother/daughter talk, the daughter pointed out that she needed feminine supplies. One never knows what impact we have when speaking out for what we believe. I can only hope that the words and actions that I felt compelled to share did more good than harm. I prayed before and during presentations and entrusted the rest to God.

At the same time I have never felt anger toward people who presented views other than the message I posed. I couldn't get caught up in pro-life or pro-abortion debates. I believed that the majority of people on both sides of the issue considered themselves promoting "the common good." I am grateful for my own experience almost two decades earlier when I wished I had postponed a D&C. It has given me empathy to listen to people's stories or regrets of choosing a pregnancy termination decision and embracing them and inviting them to name their terminated child. I became aware of how in this very Catholic community, Catholic women out-numbered others in having abortions. Often these women or affected men spoke of wishing they could talk to parents or their spouse about their past, though find some peace and reconciliation in telling someone who can listen and pray with them.

Sister Nathaniel's advice when I was graduating from eighth grade, that "nothing so terrible will ever happen in life to prevent good from resulting" took on a face. Sister emphasized that God is present in all things. Just as God embraces me where I am at, so must I do to others. The sexual revolution impacted me, my marriage, and our parenting. Don and I did our best to be open with the children on sex and drug issues.

As years went by I realized I was again bargaining with God. A part of me wanted to hope that if we were active in promoting values that we believed in, our children would get through their teen and young adult years without making choices that would weigh heavily on us and our children. We would tell them that as teenagers they were already parenting. That choices they made as teens and young adults would affect how open and transparent they could be with their children in the future.

In looking back I realize that ours was and is an average family. We were blessed with discovering marijuana in our children's possession and a pregnancy before marriage. Both were heartbreaking at the time, though later I questioned; "Who did I think I was to be above these learning opportunities?" The grandbaby was and continues to be a precious delight.

Usually I was the one to first learn of the children's offenses. I had watched Carol Burnett on a TV talk show, talking about her response to her child's drug use, and she advised that if children are living at home, regardless of their age, the parent had the right look through children's rooms, et cetera, if there is reason to believe the child is showing signs of poor judgment. This coincided with a friend calling me and asking if I would check my child's vehicle to see if her child's watch was in the car. My child had ridden to work with a co-worker, which was unusual, so the car was in the driveway. I checked. The car was unlocked though the glove compartment was locked.

Normally I would not have looked into the new high school graduate's glove compartment but Carol Burnett's words rung in my ears. I was afraid of what I might find. The car keys were lying on the floor of the car. Sure enough, there was a pot pipe in the glove compartment. My stomach tightened. I couldn't look any further, afraid I would also find marijuana.

The child got home from work before his dad did and I confronted him saying that I expected him to be the one to tell his dad before he left for the county fair that evening. If he didn't I would have to be the one to tell his dad. My brother, Kevin, was on vacation from the seminary and spending time with us. It was awkward handling the logistics calmly with Kevin in the living room.

To my surprise, when Don got home, the child asked if the two of them could go off to our bedroom. The child was unaware that I had called Don at work to give him a heads up. I knew Don well enough to know that he did best with a little time to rehearse his response. After a while I knocked on the bedroom door and was invited in as Don was explaining to our child that; "This was once — if it happened again there would be no more living at home." Our other children deserved a better example. The two men embraced. I asked if I could keep the pipe for the memory box. Request granted, though I kept it in a separate box hidden away.

Kelly provided challenges, too. She frequently

came home after her curfew. A suggestion was to shorten her curfew five minutes for every minute she was late. We decided to give it a try. She seemed to accept the new plan gracefully. The next time she came home extra late, she nonchalantly informed us that the following weekend she would simply stay home all weekend and did so without a fuss. We learned to ask our children when they would be home. They usually surprised us and came home earlier. If later than what they told us, they named their own consequences. Some of our stress was lifted.

Kelly worked as a waitress at Perkins for a couple of years. On weekends she worked until two a.m. One night she came home so upset because an African-American came in and was seated in a booth. The manager instructed her to just ignore the black person. Kelly was furious. My brother's family was black. She gave her notice. On the last night of work she came home several hours late and went to bed. Shortly thereafter she got up and called her dad out to the kitchen. Don stayed calm as she explained that she had side-swiped a police car when leaving the Perkin's parking lot and continued on to a party without notifying the police. Her dad coached her to call the police at 5:00 a.m. and explain her actions. The police had already picked up one of her teenaged co-workers who knew the circumstances but withheld the information.

Don and Kelly were instructed to go to the police station to begin whatever paper work was necessary. No charges were filed. A claim was submitted to our insurance company. And Kelly was on her way, with a clean record to begin employment at the Country Manor Nursing Home in Sartell.

Kelly, like most teens, went on to make choices that concerned her parents. I had a repeating dream of trying to spank her butt though could only get within two to three inches of contact. I interpreted that dream to mean that I feared she was headed for some regrettable trouble but that we, her parents, were unable to get her attention. Thankfully she made it to adulthood in one piece even after she and a girlfriend accepted a ride in the back of a stranger's van. She also had a red Pinto and was giving her then-boyfriend a ride home from church when we get a call at the church kitchen that she had been in an accident. She drove through a stop sign into an intersection and the front end of her car was ripped off by a car that had the right-of-way. Kelly's car was totaled. No one was hurt. "Thank you, God."

Add a few more teenagers to this mix and we had more cars totaled and more drug incidences, with a major alcohol and drug party at our house in our absence. Another college student was home for Christmas break and wanted his dad to upholster a sofa for his dorm room. Don wanted to have the job done at the prison so arranged for his sweet child to meet him at the Reformatory to choose fabric. A few days later, the child was still in bed. I had information for him to mail so went to the coat closet and pulled his gloves from his coat pocket intending to put the information and gloves together on the counter so both would be remembered.

A small white plastic sample Rose Milk lotion container fell to the floor. Again I heard Carol Burnett's voice. I popped the lid off and you probably guessed it: a small amount of marijuana. I went directly to the sleeping nineteen-year-old's bed and told him what I found and he knew the routine. He would have to talk to his dad. Darn kids! This time, I was able to be more calm.

The greatest fear for me has been when the children become depressed. Several of them have had close friends and schoolmates that have died by suicide. Depression frightens me.

Chapter Twenty-nine

In addition to aging parents, our mid-life years were filled with activity. At times I sought counseling just for guidance on how to stay sane and grounded in the midst of chaos. Sometimes Don and I went to counseling together. It was always reassuring to learn that what we were experiencing was pretty normal. Related books and a bit of advice would help to get us on track again. Sometimes I would move forward with a gut feeling as the result of my mother's words of wisdom on my wedding day; "Be sure to meet your own emotional and physical needs better than I did."

When I was being a full-time mom with no income of my own I would tend to go through periods of lack of self worth, even though it took plenty of orchestrating and organizing to keep the family running smoothly. One Valentine's Day I invited Don out to dinner at the Swan Café in Waite Park. He always paid for our dates and he appeared uncomfortable when I asked for the check and using the household checking account I paid the bill, writing at the bottom of the check "Happy Valentine's Day!" Whether he saw what I wrote or not, it made me feel like I was making a romantic financial contribution to our relationship. I think he left the tip.

    Since early marriage Don and I got away by ourselves one or two weekends a year. Again, if hotels were involved, Don paid that bill. I found myself longing for weekends of rest and relaxation. When he paid for our lodging, meals and entertainment, I had a sense that he anticipated sex as a priority on such getaways. I tried to explain how I felt, but sometimes actions speak louder than words. One of those weekends I informed him that I had enough money in the grocery account that I'd like to pay for the lodging. Perhaps this was the only thing that changed was mindset. I felt comfortable just hanging out with him with no sexual expectations. What a relief. And if copulation didn't happen at the hotel, it did after we got home. Our relationship was maturing. We shared this information as presenters to a Marriage Encounter group.

    Another time, when Don was very busy holding down two jobs and bringing in a good living he informed me that our little yard-shed needed painting and that was something I could do. I had a sense that he believed his work was important and my job was to take care of the menial labor in our life. Gloria Steinem was showing the world life from a woman's point of view. While I wasn't totally into the women's lib movement, I could relate to some of the thinking of "What is good for the goose is good for the gander."

    One day I knew I was in trouble when Don asked for postage stamps to mail his business bills. I started beating on him, out of control. He crouched and crossed his arms over his head and chest. When he left for work I called the local Mental Health Center. I had never been there before and was told I could get an appointment in two weeks. I told the receptionist to forget it, I was pre-menstrual and in two weeks life would look totally different. If a man did the abusing he would be reported to the authorities. What I did was a sign of something wrong. I wanted help immediately. The receptionist asked to put my name on a list and would call if they had a cancellation. A day later I got the call and went in.

I told the therapist that I was pre-menstrual and troubled by my thoughts and behavior. I wanted help. First the therapist told me there had recently been a case in England where a woman was acquitted of murdering her husband because she was pre-menstrual. I didn't want that to be an excuse for my behavior. It was determined that I wanted my contribution to our family to be acknowledged by Don. The therapist asked what I thought of painting the outside shed as Don requested, with the agreement that Don would pay me. I was on board. Also, I knew that I needed Don to buy his own stamps because I knew when I had stamps for the household bills and if he used them I'd be left in a lurch and frustrated.

Don accompanied me to the second and final therapy session. He agreed to pay fifty dollars for the paint job and purchase his own stamps. Sometimes minor tweaks in communication can lead to mutual respect. It worked for us.

Socially Challenged

I was getting better at identifying what emotional and spiritual needs I had to have met without seeking professional help. A son's fiancée called off their wedding two days prior to the scheduled big event. Calling the guests was like dealing with a death. The wedding was to be in the southern part of the state. The gowns and tuxedos were ordered and purchased in St. Cloud. They were all at our house waiting to be transported south. We got the wedding cancellation news on Thursday. By Monday I felt like I was a candidate to be admitted to two-south, the mental ward at the St. Cloud Hospital.

My acquired coping skills lead to me calling Don at work and informing him that I needed to stop the world and get off for a couple of days. I had loads and loads of laundry sorted. I was leaving them for the family to do. I would return the dresses to the bridal shop and tuxes to Metzroth's Men's Clothing Store before checking into a local hotel, which one; I didn't know. I packed a few essentials and an ice chest of healthy food and was on my way into St. Cloud. By the time I negotiated the returns to the clothing stores and checked into the Sunwood Inn, I was light-headed and exhausted. I hung the "Do Not Disturb" sign on the door to my room and crawled in bed, nude. Free!

After crashing for several hours I got dressed and ventured down to the dining room. It felt freeing and refreshing to order alone with plans to pay the bill with the family grocery money. A couple I recognized, also involved with the Family Life Bureau, were the only other customers in the restaurant on this Monday evening. We discussed my self-inflicted time-out. Heaven only knew what they were thinking. After lounging by the pool for a short time I returned to my room and crashed for the night.

The next morning I ate yogurt and fruit from the ice chest. After doing some stretches, showering and getting dressed, I walked a few blocks to the Cathedral Church for noon mass. My good friend, Nancy, was at mass. We rode in her vehicle to the Family Life Bureau offices. The two of us went to lunch before I returned to the hotel, still dizzy and shaky.

My room door was locked and chained shut but someone unlocked the door and then left. I learned later that the almost-groom had driven around town from hotel to motel looking for his mother's car. Perhaps he asked someone to check if I was alright. I never asked.

After a nap I called Don at work and told him where I was and would he care to join me for dinner. His question: "Are you sure?" I was sure. He said he would go home and change clothes and be back for dinner.

During dinner I asked him how the guys at work reacted to the idea of my taking a break. I was surprised to learn that he was too embarrassed to mention it to anyone. Then he asked; "If you needed to get away, why didn't you call your sister to see if she would go to a Minnesota Twins baseball game with you?" He was thinking like a man. I needed alone time, peace and quiet with no family decisions or issues. His radar and mine were planets apart. I paid for the dinner. Then I asked him if he would like to spend the night. Again he hesitantly questioned: "Are you sure?" Again; I was sure. It was obvious that his ego had been bruised and I would have to proceed with compassion. Once back to the room we readied for bed and held each other close with no expectations.

The following morning Don went back to work. I stayed in the room until check-out time. I arrived home to a most welcomed surprise. The loads of laundry were all washed, folded and put away. The house was immaculate. Someone had shopped for groceries and a pot roast was cooking. To this day I don't know who did what. I only know that taking care of my needs led to attitude adjustments, especially with the men in the family.

A few weeks later I read an article in the St. Cloud *Times* about a Cold Spring woman, like me, a mother of five children. She had gone on strike. There was a picture in the paper of the woman sitting under an umbrella in her front yard displaying a sign that read "ON STRIKE" for passers-by to see. I don't remember how long she remained on strike. When I pointed out the article to Don, He told me he had seen it a couple of weeks earlier. I asked why he hadn't shared it with me. He said that I had enough of my own ideas.

Life went on. We were concerned about RJ, who was living out-of-state, wondering how he was doing with his wedding plans changed. He came home frequently and doted on his family. I had a garage sale on my birthday weekend in October. We went, in the rain, to the Sartell football game. I was tired and drenched and decided to go home. Don looked at me with a silly smirk on his face and told me I couldn't go home yet. That made me suspicious so I remained awhile longer. Finally I was so chilled that I left. I arrived home to a house full of people. RJ had run up his phone bill by arranging a surprise birthday party for me. I took it as his way of saying "Thanks" for standing by him through some of his difficult times.

A few weeks later would be Thanksgiving. I soon realized Don wasn't a total convert to the idea of husbands and wives sharing roles. With several of the children coming home for the holiday I mentioned to Don that since the children were no longer home, I was going to need assistance with food preparations. That was foreign to him even though his dad did major cooking for family events. Don was adamant that holidays were his days to rest and the food preparations were my responsibility. I said nothing to anyone except to make reservations at Michael's Restaurant on Highway 10 in St. Cloud.

Holiday meal time was drawing near and I was bombarded with questions. I told the family that all was under control. I had a surprise for them. We were to be somewhere special at noon. Needless to mention, conversation over dinner was minimal, mostly how bland the food tasted. RJ announced that in the future he didn't care if we had turkey for Thanksgiving, pork roast would be fine and he would help prepare the food. Don was converted, too.

Around that same time Don's uncle passed away. I packed luggage for Don and myself to stay the night before the funeral in Grand Rapids. The morning of the funeral Don was getting dressed and discovered that he had no dress trousers. At first he accused me of not bringing trousers along for him. I thought the jacket and trousers were on the same hanger in the closet at home. It took only a moment for me to ask, "Why do I pack for you anyway?" There was no argument. It was simply a statement. We went shopping for trousers. I haven't done his packing for a quarter of a century. I went from being my mother to being Millie. Little did I know, Don prefers to do his own packing.

This mutual respect movement came back at me as well. With children leaving home we returned to what Don was accustomed to with his roommates prior to marriage. So I prepared the meals and he cleaned the kitchen afterwards. One evening he cleaned off the table and replaced the crocheted doily and centerpiece. He was busy at the sink. I thought he was unaware of what I was doing as I adjusted the doily to the way I usually arranged it. He turned around, no words, and adjusted it back to his way of doing it. I smiled and left it.

Together we decided that if he was learning to do housework I needed to learn how to change oil on my car. One Saturday he was working in the garage and guided me to drive my diesel-fueled Oldsmobile up on ramps. I was wearing shorts and a tank top and slid under the car on my back. Don continued to talk me through loosening the nut and bolt on the oil pan for the old oil to drain out. I don't remember all that was involved, I just remember him laughing so hard when a gust of wind caused yucky oil to lather me from head to hips. That was my last attempt to change oil. In a short time Don decided that there was no reason for either of us to change oil. Leave it to the garage guys. This decision was mostly due to the fact that state and federal laws were created at that time regulating the disposal of petroleum products. Such products now had to be taken to drop-off locations.

    Los Angeles driving gave me confidence in my driving abilities. Since moving to Minnesota, when the two of us are in the vehicle, Don usually drives and I sit in the passenger seat. I can be an excellent navigator when necessary. One day, on our way to the Twin Cities, I mentioned to Don that I felt the need to get my driving confidence back and I would like to be the chauffeur that day. He seemed to welcome the arrangement. However, nearing home, I was in the left turn lane, awaiting oncoming traffic over the Sauk Rapids Bridge. Don commented; "You could have gone instead of waiting for that car, you know." Although I remained silent, I was ticked off.

    After sorting out in my head what I was feeling, later that evening I verbally took Don back to his comment at the bridge. I asked him if he was riding with his partner from work with the same left turn scenario, would he have made a comment to his partner about a turn decision. When he answered; "No," I felt calm and confident in telling him that I would appreciate the same respect.

We have learned so much about mutual respect and communication over the years, yet how easy it is to fall back into old habits. One thing we have learned is that if the old demons raise their horns, we don't panic or fear for our relationship. We recognize that it is time to take or give space before discussing something that might be weighing on our hearts.

Way back in the "Women's Rights" literature someone was quoted as saying that in a lifetime a woman needs three husbands: one for sex, one for children, and one to grow old with and if she is lucky she will get all three in one. I suspect the same holds true for men. However, I don't accept that it is luck. Marriage, family, communication and mutual respect require hard work, ongoing learning, getting outside help if necessary and a spiritual commitment. I do feel lucky, no, fortunate, to be at this point in my life.

Chapter Thirty

*S*ometime around 1980, a surprise parcel arrived in our mailbox. The return address indicated that my friend Yola, from West Covina, had sent it. It was a Sacred Heart Church cookbook. We lived in that community and worshipped at Sacred Heart for only three years. It was a joy to recognize the names of so many people who had submitted recipes, some tempting. On page 142 there was a recipe entitled; "Millie's Dish." Yola had entered the recipe for the no name shepherd's pie casserole that she asked for when we invited their family for dinner following the death of their son, Peter. It was my version of the recipe that the mother from the pre-school group had given me years earlier.

    I was stunned. While the ingredients Yola included in the entry were those I verbally gave to her a decade earlier, my updated version had changed drastically. I was both embarrassed and honored that she named the recipe after me. My family had grown, so portions I used had increased. I was also using healthier ingredients for cooking foods. I graduated to using top quality beef. The canned green beans were replaced with frozen or fresh green beans. The Campbell's tomato soup became tomato sauces, stewed tomatoes or even fresh tomatoes. The milk sometimes was soy milk. Early on I may have even used instant mashed potatoes, especially if camping. Later I peeled, boiled and mashed Russet potatoes. Eventually I boiled unpeeled red potatoes and mashed them. The cheeses that top the mashed potatoes varied from event to event according to what ingredients I had on hand and my mood.

Gradually, "Millie's Dish" turned into fodder for personal meditations and discernment. We are all given a foundation or recipe for life. Influences, circumstances and experiences along the way alter our outlook on life. As for me, there is a part of my core beliefs and traditions I continue to adhere to. I cherish how my Catholic tradition and family life offer me a sense of being grounded. I seek out learning experiences, travel and challenges that give me a deeper appreciation of God's love for all of creation. My recipe for life also continues to change depending on life's ingredients and situations.

During the seventies, eighties and nineties so many opportunities for broadening my horizons presented themselves. I welcomed affiliating myself with being on the cutting edge of bringing new opportunities to the community. In addition to diocesan family life and parish work, I thrived on being a teen advocate. Don and I were on the committees to bring all-night lock-in graduation parties to the Sartell community.

Millie Hoelscher Moran

Don, being a car guy, assumed the task of approaching a car dealer with children attending Sartell High School to donate a used car, in good condition, for the top prize drawing at the end of the party at six-o'clock a.m. Now, nearly thirty years later, we live across the street from SHS and each graduation party a used car, in good condition, continues to be displayed in front of the school and given away at the grad party.

Both Don and I were on the committee to get band trips started for SHS students. I was on the planning and events committee plus a chaperone for the first band trip in 1977. We took one hundred and six students in three buses to Disney World in Orlando. It was very humid that June day at Disney with our kids in their warm, woolen St. Paul Winter Carnival-weight uniforms. The school was only about ten years old and the heavy weight uniform was the only option the band had at the time.

Other bands had marchers drop out due to heat. We were proud of our kids and grateful to the Cold Spring band parents who coached us in many aspects of being on tour with bands. The salt tablets and water bottles we used while walking alongside band members squirting water into marcher's mouths kept every participant in the vertical position until the Disney parade was over. My group of girls was assigned to go to a cool dreary room behind the scenes of Disney to cool off and regroup. Lynn, one of the SHS marchers, lay down on the concrete floor next to the floor drain and pulled open her wool jacket. She had absolutely no clothing on under her wool jacket. That must have been itchy. I admired her tenacity and envied her bust-line.

Our family hosted two exchange students from Japan and one from France during the children's teen years. We benefited in ways of human and cultural relations. Sometimes I was less than proud of the way our children treated the students. They pretty much ignored them. The students' interactions were with me more than any other family member. My children's behavior was probably typical for many teenagers.

When Keith was a preschooler I had hoped to get both him and me into the Seaton Hall parenting and preschooler program in St. Cloud. The year we were to begin, the fee for people outside of St. Cloud was raised to a level I could not justify. Moved by the Spirit, I sought ways to begin a program in Sartell. I envisioned a program based on the one I had experienced in California, only this one would offer a spiritual twist. My children babysat for Nancy Knapp, a school teacher. She had preschoolers and was interested in assisting in getting the program off the ground. My own parish pastor was open to the program though St. Francis had no available daytime space.

With Father Kleinschmidt's support and encouragement, Nancy, who belonged to the Riverside Presbyterian Church in Sartell made the necessary contacts with her pastor and the two of us were scheduled to meet with their governing body, The Session. We did so. Again we received tremendous support for an organization that we called the Sartell Christian

Millie Hoelscher Moran

Family Development Program. A gentleman from Riverside built us a supply cabinet. We put announcements in church bulletins and to our amazement we had eighteen moms with children. My heart was pounding that first meeting day as I used the keys entrusted to me by the Presbyterian Session. The group was too large for discussions, so we split the group and offered it on two different days each week. This was a volunteer position.

Parents donated toys, puzzles and art supplies for the program. I provided the discussion topics and discussion leadership and a family and child development check-out library. Other mothers took turns providing beverages and snacks. Moms would also take their turn at supervising the youngsters during discussion time. The community was small enough that mothers and children developed relationships that continue today. By the second year, two elderly Notre Dame Sisters, residing at the St. Francis Xavier convent, assumed the supervision of children so all mothers could participate in the discussions.

Being comfortable in the larger community and with staff at the public school, I contacted the district to see if they would like to offer their eighth grade home economics students the opportunity to observe our preschoolers and record behavior back to the home economics/ family living teacher. Each student would be assigned to one preschooler. The school board approved and busses transported participating eighth graders to and from the church for several weeks.

Socially Challenged

For many decades the policy in Minnesota was for public school students to be released one hour a week to their various churches for religion classes. The law was still in effect though religion classes were eventually held on Wednesday evenings for public school students. My friend Nancy Moran and I again approached the school board to get approval to use the accumulated legal allotment of time to take eleventh and twelfth graders from our respective parishes on two retreats a year during school hours, without students being considered absent as long as parents signed a permission slip and paid a nominal fee for the bus trips and speakers at places like Newman Center, St. Francis Retreat Center In Little Falls or Crosier Seminary in Onamia, Minnesota.

Nancy and I racked our brains as to activities to keep our students' attention. Several times we arranged for Jack Quesnell, licensed marriage and family therapist from the Twin Cities, to present to our group. He was always well-received. When Nan and I would brainstorm, we'd walk away from the session not knowing who had what idea. Our ideas simply meshed. We sensed the Spirit was at work. One spring we arranged for MaMa Di, from MaMa Di's Restaurant, in St. Paul, to be the guest presenter at Crosier Seminary in Onamia. MaMa had a reputation for feeding the poor, especially on the feast of St. Joseph, March 19. Every year on that feast day she opened her eatery and fed throngs of people in the inner city for free. I liked her message of when people gave her bouquets of roses; she would keep one rose for herself and share the rest with shut-ins or residents of nursing facilities.

In the midst of parenting pre-teen to adult children, my dad turned into an old man, his body ravaged by multiple sclerosis. Following is the poem which I wrote and read at his funeral, December 13, 1983.

A Daughter's Prayer
There was a couple
A man and wife
Some might think they had a difficult life.
They knew financial struggles
As most couples do
Along with parenting pains
As children chose their own values.
As time went on and good health began to decline
It was plain to see it was just a matter of time
That one spouse or both would be called from this life.
Only God knew which would go first . . . the man or his wife.
The man suffered physically and emotionally
As his body gave way to MS
The wife suffered too as she met the challenge of this test.
Children and loved ones stood by and felt sad
How would you feel if you fell on your dad?
When the man was taken from this world
to the angels above
I whispered a prayer.
"Thank you, Lord, for this lesson in love"

Socially Challenged

Both Nancy and I had heard Leo Buscaglia, Ph.D., a lecturer from California, also known for his many books on loving, learning and living. We liked his message in lectures, books and film. We decided to incorporate Leo's film into that one-day retreat. We promoted the event as "Love Italian Style" with MaMa Di in person and include Leo Buscaglia's videos. The Crosier students joined our bus load and a couple of station-wagons full of Saint Francis and Saint Stephen students and chaperones. The Crosiers provided the facility and an Italian-style noon meal. Nancy ordered a couple of cases of Catawba grape juice to give more of an Italian ambiance. Don took off work for the day to be a chauffeur/ chaperone. Since we didn't send the children to St. Cloud Cathedral for a Catholic education, we dedicated ourselves to providing spiritual/relational experiences that might leave a positive impression on the young people. Just like Don's corrections job, there was no way to know what impact our presence in their lives might have.

We had to learn a few things about when to schedule summer teen events. If we scheduled a post-confirmation party before football or other sports practices began, the chance of someone bringing alcohol was greater than after teens had signed their code of ethics agreement with their schools in late August. When we lived on the Mississippi River we thoroughly enjoyed those parties. Parents assisted by bringing food for a picnic meal and a few adults with boats offered kids opportunities to learn how to water ski. It was a thrill to observe a teen's confidence shine through the smiles on their faces when they finally accomplished the water-skiing feat.

Some years we'd rent a cabin for a week at Agate Lake, near Nisswa. The resort was owned by my oldest female cousin, Irene, and her family. Kids staying at the resort would bring a couple of dollars to Don to help pay for boat gas. Our family worked with strangers to learn to water-ski. Our son Lee was so patient with the kids. If the youngsters were unable to master skiing, Lee would offer them the opportunity to ski while wearing a life jacket and standing on Lee's feet. Lee, also wearing a life jacket, would hang on to the ski rope with one hand and wrap his forearm around his young passenger. What joy for all of us!

The resort offered a volleyball court. Our family would go through the resort recruiting players. Don and I participated with the young people. Other parents asked if we were teachers because of the way we interacted with the youth. One year on Friday, the day before leaving, we passed the word to the other cabin dwellers that we would welcome all to join our family for a potluck supper in the common area. We had an awesome response. The year of our twenty-fifth wedding anniversary, Irene agreed to keep an eye on our two youngest children while we took the day for ourselves. Upon our return we were notified to be in the common area about five-thirty for a potluck supper. To our surprise some of the avid fishing people were deep-frying hundreds of sunfish. Irene and Darrell provided a case of champagne to celebrate Don and me.

We were not planning to celebrate our milestone anniversary because Kelly was married two weeks earlier. We were in for another surprise. Our children arranged for a surprise twenty-fifth anniversary party at our home for the day after we returned from the cabin.

As the older children were getting married and starting families, I sought various ways to fill my life. Several of the children lived out of state and away from St. Cloud. My own decorating business provided good income though I desired more. One day a week for eight years I volunteered in the hospital's surgery lounge. Involvement in health care situations continued to be fulfilling. Supporting and enjoying people continues to be a major ingredient of Millie's Spiritual Dish. When Keith attended the University of St. Thomas in St. Paul, I took advantage of the opportunity for parents to take classes free. Twice a week I drove the ninety-eight miles to continue my education in the environment that three of the children received their college degrees. I loved philosophy classes. My only regret was when a professor kept emphasizing in a 101 level class that abortion was wrong. I had the opportunity to speak up and express my thoughts on how that topic needed more discussion which might lead to offering support to anyone who might have been experiencing some level of post-abortion trauma. I was too timid and I am sorry.

For the past three of our Moran Christmas celebrations our children decided they want to remain close to their Twin Cities homes and keep the holiday meal simple. They created an annual lasagna contest. The host household supplies the essentials and the four other families bring lasagna. Don and I would be assigned a salad or whatever the host couple preferred. This past Christmas, with grandchildren married and with children, our numbers were up to thirty-five. Don and I requested a qualifying lasagna pan. We prepared our ingredients on Christmas Eve at home and on the big day managed to get our lasagna pan into one of the ovens without the family realizing what we brought. When the foil was raised off of the five lasagna pans, several voices from two generations proclaimed in unison, "Millie's Dish!"

    While the extra food and memorable family recipe was well-received, it did not win the "Favorite Lasagna" vote. That award went to Rachel, the newest in-law. She took home the roaming winner's plaque and is entitled to host next year's Moran Family Christmas. It will be interesting how that plays out. Rachel and Keith live in a small house that cannot accommodate thirty-five family members.

Epilogue

The last chapter was written nine months ago. Perhaps crippled by writer's block, philosophically closing the final chapter to this first book plagued me. I prayed and tried to discern ways of bringing it to fruition. The birth of a grandchild, the wedding of our oldest grandson and our major involvement in the local Alzheimer's Chapter and support group kept my mind and energies focused elsewhere. Raising funds for the annual Alzheimer's walk, related speaking engagements, including a first for me, a live radio-interview, and ordering and reading dementia related books kept me busy. Don and I feel fortunate to be living now compared to people only a decade ago who suffered with dementia. There is still no known effective cure or treatment for this dreaded disease, though research and knowledge of the brain has become a societal priority. The Alzheimer's Association, support groups and books aid us in becoming informed about the disease both as the diagnosed and the care partner.

October 2012 erupted with a welcomed balance to our lives that opened the door to finalizing this writ-

Millie Hoelscher Moran

ing work in progress. It had been awhile since we had attended concerts. Our comfort level driving in the Twin Cities or taking vacations had diminished. We have learned to surround ourselves with companion travelers and drivers. The local Paramount Theatre and Saint Kate's O'Shaughnessey Auditorium in St. Paul had three concerts scheduled within three weeks. I got online and purchased tickets for all three. The first and third concerts here in St. Cloud we could handle on our own. The second we invited my brother, Lloyd, who was born three weeks after we were married and his wife, Sharon to accompany us. All three performances became the ingredients for integrating the three separate significant phases of my individual life into one.

    The first, Mathew and Gunnar, twin sons of Ricky Nelson, grandsons of "Ozzie and Harriet Nelson" brought to St. Cloud their show "Remembering Ricky Nelson," their rock star dad who was killed in a plane crash when the twins, now age forty-five, were eighteen years old. I compare my formative years to Disneyland's Mad Tea Cup Party ride that served as supporting and holding my early life values in place as I breathed the air of the world beyond family traditions. The weekly, wholesome Nelson family show was a part of that ride. The second concert was the three Minnesota liturgical music writers who provided worldwide worship lyrics and music that stirred the attention of young people and ourselves when we worked with teens back in the '70s, '80s and '90s following Vatican II. The three were Father Michael Joncas, David Haas and Marty Haugen. Like the Nelsons, Pat Boone appeared live here in St. Cloud, ten minutes from home and reminiscing about life and music in the '60s and '70s.

Like their famous dad, the Nelson twins, singing Rick's songs, invited members of the audience to come up after the show for autograph signing. They also invited stories about their dad to help them better understand his and their family's lives. The twins shared stories that people at other shows had told them. Don and I decided to tell the guys about when Don was the foreman at an upholstery shop on Lankershim Boulevard in North Hollywood, California, and their mother's station wagon was brought into the shop. Chris, their mom, wanted the cloth fabric seats to be replaced with vinyl. We assumed this was for child proofing reasons. Gunnar assured us that it was not for child proofing but rather, their mother had taken a cooking class and was transporting a container of her favorite recipe, *cioppino* (Italian fish soup) in her vehicle and slammed on the brakes at a changing intersection light with fish soup everywhere. Whether their mother would tell the same version of the incident is anybody's guess.

We thoroughly enjoyed our interaction with these guys. It gave substance to and legitimized our own existence in California. We've been gone four decades and that life seemed totally disconnected to life here in Minnesota. Gunnar and Matthew's version of their mom's episode of slamming on the brakes at a California intersection happened about the same time as my own similar California station wagon incident. Most vehicles in the United States didn't even have seatbelts at that time. Lee was about four years old with the seats down in the back of my station wagon which allowed for Lee to move about while playing with his hot wheels. I came to an intersection at Valley Boulevard in Alhambra a bit too fast as the light turned yellow and braked to a stop. The veterinarian's office where I was to pick up Mitzi, the family poodle, was just to the left of the intersection. Lee slid forward, gashing his scalp on the ashtray in the back of the front backrest. Bleeding and tears were minimal so I proceeded to pick up the dog before taking Lee fifteen miles in the opposite direction to our family physician for suturing the cut. To my surprise the veterinarian offered to put in a couple of sutures at no charge. I agreed. A welcomed gesture appreciated by a busy mother.

Pat Boone brought to the local audience his now somewhat gravelly voice that contrasted his young mellow voice playing in the background with 1950s '60s black and white images on a dropped screen. His theme now was God, family and patriotism. I purchased his book, Pat Boone's *America: 50 Years* autobiography. On the way home in the car, I began, in true Millie fashion, paging back to front through his book. Page 123 has a heading, "A Right to Life." Pat goes into describing the day that his daughter, Debbie, then age fifteen, came home from her Beverly Hills private school, sobbing. After parental concern and prodding

Debbie told them that at her school's science fair that day babies were in bottles and the teacher referred to them as fetuses, not babies. Debbie insisted they were babies with eyes, nose, fingers, and so on. Pat tells that it was this incident that lead to the Boone Family becoming advocates for the unborn in California and later beyond.

Tears gushed uncontrollable from deep within me. I was with the Southern California Right to Life League's Speaker's Bureau in the early 1970s as legalized therapeutic abortion was being touted and voted into law in California. Each time I prepared to enter a school with the containers of babies at various pre-birth developmental stages, I begged God's love of the young high school students and me to get us through this in a positive way. As mentioned earlier in this book, I was concerned about the effect the display of these unborn babies might have on youth. After forty plus years, learning of Debbie and the Boone Family's response to the Right to Life's approach to teaching society about pre-birth human development I was gifted with the affirmation I longed for though had stuffed it deep into the recesses of my memory. What Pat doesn't mention and what I believe is that those babies were not legally or illegally aborted babies, though because they were formed perfectly were likely the result of a spontaneous abortion (natural miscarriage). Just like no seatbelts were in cars in that era, spontaneous abortions happened naturally and were disposed of differently than they are today.

Millie Hoelscher Moran

****

A huge eye-opener for me this past week in the midst of the final days prior to 2012 presidential election and all of the pro-life, pro-marriage issues discussed on talk shows and TV ads, projecting that the Democrats are considered the liberals and the Republicans are billed as the conservatives. I woke up one morning feeling compelled to log on to my computer to check who was President when Roe v. Wade was passed. Richard Nixon, a Republican, was president. Then I checked for the Supreme Court Justices to refresh my memory as to the political aspirations of the high court at that time. Three Democratic Judges and four Republican judges (three elevated to that status by President Nixon) voted in legalized abortion. Now my head is surely spinning. Society has changed so much in forty years.

    A few days later I decided to research the name Rose Polito, a 1970 Southern California Right to Life League activist. Rose Polito and Libby Goodwin were listed as significant players in the adoption of this educational league. Both women had been in our West Covina, California, home helping to get pre-birth education going in the San Gabriel Valley area. I had just graduated from high school as a thirty-two year old and chose to make this ministry as my vocation as long as it fit into family life demands. The same group of pro-lifers arranged to have doctors John and Lyn Billings from Australia to Southern California. Saturated with human fertility information from both of these sources prepared me for the work I would eventually be involved in when we moved back to Minnesota in 1972.

In retrospect, the '60s and '70s, during what I considered a wonderful time in my life in California, President Kennedy, Robert Kennedy and Martin Luther King all gave their lives for what they believed to be The Common Good. The Cuban Missile Crisis rattled our country to its core. The counter-cultural drug and sexual revolution took hold. The Vietnam War divided our country with repercussions lingering today. Roe v. Wade became law and continues to divide the nation. Moved by history our country will choose leadership in a few days. Lord, be with us. I choose to trust that whatever the outcome, in the grand scheme of things life will go on and pain and growth are all part of the same package.

****

This past October 12 I telephoned Robert, youngest son of my friend Yola, in West Covina, California. Yola and I both had birthdays in October. Grieving, Robert informed me that his mother passed away September 30 and was buried a few days earlier. Then I grieved. My longtime California connection had slipped into the next stage of life that is unknown. Another significant California earthly connection was severed. Peace be with you, Yola.

Don recently got his results on his neurological tests done a month earlier. We both had a sense that his cognitive skills had changed since his first test two years ago. He has had a couple of days of tears mixed in with the rest of his activities. It was a little death and more grieving for both of us. John, one of the young-onset Alzheimer's people in our Alzheimer's support group uses the cliché "What choice do we have but to play the cards that were dealt to us?" This is not a good analogy in Don's case. He has always considered himself unlucky in anything competitive. I remind him we have been lucky in our relationship, even though it has been hard work and dedication.

The first day or so Don had to wrestle with anger regarding his officially joining the ranks of diagnosed dementia that could lead to Alzheimer's, versus care partner in our Memory Loss Support Group. I tried to reassure him that we have been advocates for things we believed in throughout our marriage and I suspect we've been called or blessed to be advocates with others like ourselves to embrace what has formerly been a stigma known as senility and now has science, the government and the Alzheimer's Association working toward research and support for the afflicted as well as support for care partners of people with dementia and Alzheimer's. Don shot back with, "In other things I have felt I had a choice; with memory loss I have no choice. I feel like it has been dumped on me."

A few days later we were able to discuss how fortunate we are to be living at this time in history compared to when our relatives were going through similar challenges. There is more hope, if not for us personally, perhaps for our children as the baby boomers are moving into their later years. The Alzheimer's numbers are likely to soar and families and government agencies are going to need a better-informed society to assist in the care of related mounting health care issues. I am grateful, too, for my diagnosis two years ago. I am the one who seeks information and support. We have a clearer picture of what may or may not happen. We've learned the dementia language. We are aware of agencies and healthcare people that will walk the walk with us and our family if we allow them to. These tools have led to the two of us learning to step back when conversations between us get garbled and use some newly learned communication skills. We could relate to others in our support group when they spoke of the tension in their marriage before the diagnosis and wondering if their marriage would end in divorce. Knowledge is power. In this case, this is the power to understand, cope and love. Our neurologist informed us last week that we, as a couple, are well ahead of the learning curve in this situation than the majority of his patients bring to the table. These are positive strokes that don't come from family or friends who know nothing of the disease.

 For some reason the events of this October have lead me to feel free of the fragmented sense I have carried with me most of my life. Rather than feeling on the fringes of other people's lives, I feel restored or glued to the core that is me while connected to all of humanity. Just as I chose and with Don's support to be on the cutting edge of various life issues in our earlier years and now in the aging process, I get a sense that while

Millie Hoelscher Moran

there will be a thousand joys and sorrows as we discover together what we are made of. God help us to not let dementia or Alzheimer's define us but aid us in growing more humanly and godly as we embrace the ambiguity.

Final Notes

Sixteen of the eighteen siblings, ranging in age of forty-nine to seventy-four, are alive today, relatively healthy and contributing members to society. The last time we were all together was at our mother's funeral five-and-a-half years ago. Mom's descendants and their spouses were instructed to gather on the steps of the church between the cemetery rituals and the luncheon for photo shoots. Over two hundred of us swarmed to the familiar gathering place.

Following the luncheon, Allen, the executor of Mom's affairs, informed us to meet at Mom's house at 2:00 p.m. for distribution of her belongings. He had us draw numbers one to seventeen (including Kevin's widow). First Al took the six sisters into Mom's bedroom, and according to our numbers we chose a piece of Mom's jewelry. Then each of the seventeen was given the opportunity to take whatever items we had given to our mother over our lifetime. Next, each of us, one to seventeen, was invited to take our turn going through the house collecting an item we would like while respecting other people's wishes. It was amazing how smoothly this played out. In true Hoelscher fashion, many members became bored with the indoor activities and headed for various areas in the neighborhood for sport's activities.

By word of mouth, Mom's house sold within a month to a rural farm woman wanting to retire in Browerville. Our lives went on, missing Mom and busy with our own families. Family wedding or graduation gatherings overwhelm me. I make token appearances at family events but prefer travel, dinner, lunch, theater or a walk in the park with an individual, couple or family. I feel blessed to be from such a large family and comfortable picking up the phone and calling anyone of them or aunts and uncles simply to just check in to hear their voices and share news. Life is good.